ADLARD COLES SHORE GUIDE

CHANNEL COAST OF FRANCE

Everything you need to know
when you step ashore

PAUL HEINEY

ADLARD COLES

LONDON · OXFORD · NEW YORK · NEW DELHI · SYDNEY

CONTENTS

How to use this book 6
Sailing to France 10
GR 34 – the Brittany
    walking route 12

THE WILD COAST OF FINISTERRE
L'ABER WRAC'H
▶ TRÉBEURDEN 14

L'Aber Wrac'h 16
Roscoff/Bloscon 19
Morlaix 22
Trébeurden 25

CÔTE DE GRANIT ROSE (THE PINK GRANITE COAST)
PERROS-GUIREC
▶ PAIMPOL 28

Perros-Guirec 30
Tréguier 32
Lézardrieux 35
Paimpol 37

CÔTE D'ÉMERAUDE (THE EMERALD COAST, INCLUDING BAIE DE ST BRIEUC)
ST QUAY PORTRIEUX
▶ ST MALO 40

St Quay Portrieux 42
Binic 45
Le Légué 48
Dahouët 50
St Cast 53
St Malo 55

▲ Roscoff/Bloscon, *page 19*

▲ St Malo, *page 55*

THE COTENTIN
PENINSULA
GRANVILLE
▶ ST VAAST 60

Granville 62
Carteret 65
Diélette 68
Cherbourg 70
St Vaast la Hougue 74

D-DAY BEACHES
OF NORMANDY
CARENTAN
▶ HONFLEUR 78

Carentan 80
Grandcamp-Maisy 83
Port-en-Bessin 86
Courseulles-sur-Mer 88
Ouistreham/Caen 92
Dives-sur-Mer 95
Deauville/Trouville 97
Honfleur 101

THE NORMANDY
AND PICARDY COAST
LE HAVRE
▶ DUNKERQUE 106

Le Havre 108
Fécamp 111
St Valery en Caux 114
Dieppe 116
Le Tréport 120
St Valery sur Somme 123
Étaples 126
Boulogne-Sur-Mer 129
Calais 133
Gravelines 136
Dunkerque 139

THE CHANNEL
ISLANDS 142

Braye – Alderney 144
St Peter Port – Guernsey 148
St Helier – Jersey 152

Index 156   Picture credits 160

▲ Braye, Alderney, *page 144*

HOW TO USE THIS BOOK

This guide starts at the western tip of France, at L'Aber Wrac'h, and heads eastwards as far as Dunkerque, just before the Belgian border. It does this for good reason: many of the harbours along the north French coast have tidal constraints: some dry completely, others have marinas with sills that can only be crossed with sufficient rise of tide. It makes sense, therefore, to work with the flood tide if you possibly can.

Wherever you might be, wait until the tide has risen far enough to allow you to be released, and you can then carry that same tide to the next harbour to arrive around high water (HW). That's the theory, anyway. As we all know, it never quite works out as comfortably as that. But on balance, from west to east is the best way to go and that is the route this book takes.

But why do you need a book like this at all? The problem is that once you have landed in France, the pilot books that got you across the Channel in safety have already done you proud. The tidetables have kept you from going aground, and speeded your passage by detailing the fast-flowing waters off the French and English coasts. But their job is now done and you can put them back on the shelf.

Also, the pilot book that has kept you to the channels and described the lights and buoys has now completed its task. You are alongside, tied up and pleased to be in harbour. Sailing is behind you and dry land beckons. This is when you need a different kind of pilot book.

Where the navigation books end is where these books, the *Adlard Coles Shore Guides*, begin. These are pilots too, but instead of guiding you past the dangers they help steer you towards the necessities and the pleasures. In my many years of cruising these waters I have found that the vast proportion of my planning has been spent in getting there, but I have given little thought to what I will do when I arrive, or even what kind of place I will end up in.

It is only when the mooring lines are ashore and the rattle of the engine is stilled that attention turns to what lies in wait. At first you will feel like a fish out of water. You need a friend to guide you, and that is the job of these books.

But don't expect to read about every harbour and anchorage in northern France. I have chosen only those where you can moor alongside in safety, and would feel happy to leave a boat

for a lengthy day while you explore ashore. The more remote anchorages and drying harbours are every bit as attractive, but the cruising can be more demanding and leave you less inclined towards a relaxed frame of mind, which exploring ashore requires.

Most sailors arriving at a new harbour find their minds suddenly filled with questions. How far are the shops? Where can I get a bite to eat? Where is the diesel, shackles,

LEGEND

🛥 Harbours visited

▦ Parc naturel marin

▦ Parc naturel régional

▦ Foreshore

═ Motorway/dual carriageway

— Main road

be the biggest or the best shops but they are the nearest. As far as walking times go, I have taken them from somewhere near the harbour offices. You will soon discover your own pace and be able to adjust the times to suit your stride. Mindful that many people cruise as a family, and children may be small, the walking distance to the nearest beach is of paramount importance. And will there be chips when you get there?

To sum up, when you've stopped the engine, tidied the deck, fixed the warps and fenders, and are wondering what to do next, that is when you should pick up this book. It doesn't claim to contain everything you might be looking for, but if it goes so far as to make your time in harbour an even more enjoyable one, then it will have done its job.

I would just add that this book was compiled during the Covid-19 pandemic, which of course restricted the amount of time I was able to spend in France. Some material has been gathered from multiple other sources, but I am confident that the information you find here will not disappoint.

water, laundry? Or just as likely, where can I find culture, entertainment, beaches, playgrounds and all the other things that a cruising crew looks forward to when the other half of cruising, the shore-side bit, takes hold?

For each harbour, I have given the briefest of descriptions from a sailing point of view – the detail is for others to provide and this is *not a book to be used for navigation* – but when planning a cruise, it is useful to sit back in the chair at home and distinguish the tricky harbours from the easy ones, and I have tried to flag these for you. I have given you distances from nearby harbours, but these are the roughest of guides, to give you a basic idea of scale.

Remembering that for most sailors their only form of transport is their own two feet, I have compiled this book from a pedestrian's point of view, and lucky you if your boat has room for bikes on board. I have tried to find the nearest supermarkets, laundries and that most important ingredient of any French cruise, the fresh morning bread and croissant. They might not

▼ Work this coastline with the tides to avoid long waits at harbour entrances. LW at St Vaast

Fécam
Étretat
Côte d'A
Cap d'Antifer
Les L
Criquetot-l'Esneval God
Cauville-sur-Mer
Octeville-sur-Mer
Montivillier
Ste-Adresse
Harfleur
LE HAVRE
L A
BAIE DE
LA SEINE
Honfleur
Côte de Nacre
Côte Fleurie
Deauville
Port-en-Bessin
Courseulles-sur-Mer
Bernières-sur-Mer
Touques
Beuzev
Bayeux
St-Aubin-sur-Mer
Langrune-sur-Mer
Villers-sur-Mer
St-Arnoult
Luc-sur-Mer
Cabourg
Houlgate
Creully
Lion-sur-Mer
Pont-l'Évêq
Thaon
Ouistreham
Dives-sur-Mer
Mathieu
Bénouville
Cormeil
Bretteville-l'Orgueilleuse
Hérouville-St-Clair
Dozulé
Le Breuil-en-Auge
Carpiquet
CAEN
Troarn
Moyau
Louvigny
Gagny
Cambremer
Lisieux
Argences
Pays d'A
Villers-Bocage
Fontenay-le-Marmion
Mézidon-Canon
u g
N O R M A N D I
St-Pierre-sur-Dives
Livarot-Pays-d'A
St-Rémy
Potigny

SAILING TO FRANCE

A 'quick flit' across the Channel used to be the easiest thing from an administrative point of view. However, the UK's departure from the European Union and the Covid-19 pandemic put a stop to that, or at least made it somewhat more problematic.

The Covid situation can be fast-changing and the procedures in place as I write could be history by the time you read this book, so the only advice is to ensure you read *up-to-date and authoritative* websites for the latest information. Check the time stamps carefully and don't rely on internet 'gossip'. I have found **gov.uk** to be the best, and equally the French government website **diplomatie.gouv.fr**. Download the NHS app to your phone so that you can save your proof of vaccination for presentation when required. TousAntiCovid is the app used in France, although the NHS app is expected to be functional too.

The arrival procedure for yachts coming to France has been simplified, but still requires forethought and planning. You must fill in an online form before arrival, and again when you leave France. You are now able to arrive at the harbour of your choice. At the time of writing, this form is just being introduced but it seems it will be available as a download from marina websites. It asks for the usual details of boat and crew, but also for proof of insurance against medical costs that

may be incurred while in France – this part is new. Again, these procedures are developing and will doubtless evolve into a system that is as trouble-free as it can possibly be. Remember, a lot of maritime businesses, including hospitality, are hugely reliant on visiting yachts and will offer all assistance.

Checklist

- Passports with six months left on them before the expiry
- Boat registration certificate (and VAT documents – see below)
- Proof of vaccination on a smartphone app that is recognisable in Europe
- Proof of the boat's insurance, and personal accident/health insurance
- Flares, liferafts etc in date
- Necessary devices to complete online forms on the go

There is also the issue of boats arriving from the UK with red (partially taxed) diesel in their tanks. Unlike the Belgians, the French have given this little attention so far. At your last fill-up in the UK, make sure you obtain a decent-looking receipt to show that what is in your tank was not bought illegally in France.

If you want to stay in France for longer than three months you must apply for a Long Stay Visa, which falls outside the scope of this book. Likewise, the VAT regulations can become exceedingly complex depending on where you want to keep your boat if outside the UK, when you bought it, and where it might have been built and tax paid in the first place. It is better to take expert and informed advice on this rather than rely on anecdotal sources, of which there are many, few of which are reliable.

GR 34 – THE BRITTANY WALKING ROUTE

This is a guide for sailors and not walkers, but as you sail both the north and south coasts of Brittany you'll keep stumbling across a remarkable walking path – the GR (Grand Rondonnée) 34.

There are more than a hundred of these carefully planned walking routes in Europe and the trails in France extend some 60,000km (37,280 miles). They all carry the same signposting – a white stripe above a red stripe. Usually they are obvious but sometimes you might have to closely examine a gatepost before you spot one. Incidentally, if you see a red strip crossed with a white stripe it means 'not this way'.

GR 34 is known as the 'customs trail' because this was a useful coastal route taken by customs officers seeking smugglers. For us, it is a chance to get some of the best sea views to be had along its 2,000km (1,240 miles); it is reckoned to be France's most popular trail.

For the purposes of this guide, we'll focus on the stretch of path that starts around L'Aber Wrac'h and takes you along the coast all the way to Mont St Michel. This is the very best stretch of French Channel coastline, taking in both the pink and the emerald granite stretches to the sandier bay of St Malo.

If you're on a boat it's doubtful you'll want to walk great lengths of it. However, it connects some harbours where you might happily leave your boat safely for an overnight to walk to the next harbour, which was perhaps not on your list of planned stops. You may be able to see and enjoy more of Brittany this way.

The GR 34 gives you an opportunity to get even deeper into this splendid part of France. Be sure to have a map on board, and good walking boots.

◄ The rugged Crozon peninsula – one of the many spectacular coastlines on this walking route

▲ Look out for the red and white GR signs – not always easy to spot

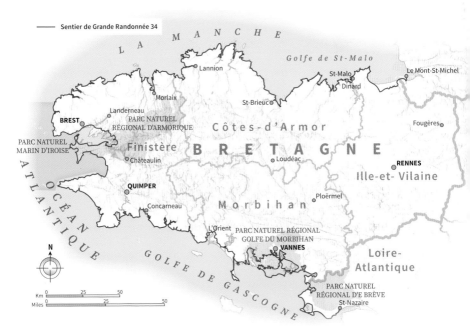

—— Sentier de Grande Randonnée 34

LA MANCHE

Golfe de St-Malo

Lannion

St-Malo

Dinard

Le Mont-St-Michel

Morlaix

St-Brieuc

Landerneau

PARC NATUREL
RÉGIONAL D'ARMORIQUE

BREST

Côtes-d'Armor

Fougères

PARC NATUREL
MARIN D'IROISE

Finistère

BRETAGNE

Châteaulin

Loudéac

Ille-et-Vilaine

RENNES

QUIMPER

Concarneau

Morbihan

Ploërmel

OCÉAN ATLANTIQUE

L'Orient

PARC NATUREL RÉGIONAL
GOLFE DU MORBIHAN

VANNES

Loire-
Atlantique

N

GOLFE DE GASCOGNE

PARC NATUREL
RÉGIONAL D'E BRÈVE

St-Nazaire

Km   0   25   50
Miles 0   25   50

THE WILD COAST OF FINISTERRE

L'ABER WRAC'H ▶ TRÉBEURDEN

THIS STRETCH OF COAST from L'Aber Wrac'h to Trébeurden can often live up to its name for ruggedness. This is that bit of the French coast that points like a finger into the Atlantic Ocean; a volatile sea that can pound this granite coastline with fury. But that's mostly in the winter.

For summer cruising this is a comforting stretch of coastline, but with a remote feel to it. In fact, there is plenty of shelter and safety to be had along the way. There is a sheltered harbour at either end, and just to be on the safe side there's a useful one halfway between, at

Roscoff. For complete shelter, there's the possibility of an upriver trip to Morlaix, an atmospheric and well-preserved medieval Breton town.

Being surrounded by the sea, shellfish and other seafood is never far from any Breton menu. They say you can catch lobsters along this coast with just a small net on a stick, and provided that you know how to pick them up without being nipped, there are crabs aplenty. Mussels are easily removed from rocks, and if you want to go digging you can find clams and cockles lurking not too far down in sandbanks. Remember the fast-moving tides if scavenging, and know the rules that protect undersized lobster and crabs. There are bans on seafood fishing at certain times of year, so ask at harbour offices. If you get the go-ahead, this activity can occupy families for hours when the weather might not be right for sailing. Add to your boat's locker a small spade and a good bucket.

This coastline gives you a real taste of Brittany, with granite rocks to baffle you when you're navigating and impressive granite buildings to gaze on ashore. And don't forget to show your appreciation for the 'Onion Johnnies' if you call into Roscoff – these sellers' pink onions are so sweet you can almost eat them like an apple.

There are anchorages along this coast that you will have to discover for yourself together with a good pilot book, and many of these have inviting beaches. But tourism is never far away on this stretch of the coast, and if you feel an urgent need for a thriving resort (and a comfortable marina) then a visit to Trébeurden will prove a refreshing finale to this wildest bit of Channel France.

▼ A timeless feel to the approaches to Roscoff

L'ABER WRAC'H

FALMOUTH 95NM, **ALDERNEY** 117NM, **MORLAIX** 40NM, **TRÉBEURDEN** 45NM

L'Aber Wrac'h lies at a crossroads and is where many Brittany adventures begin or end. It's a perfect landfall if heading south from the UK, and a good stop-over if you've been cruising south Brittany and are heading back home. It is also the perfect place to start a Channel cruise of the northern coast of France and carry the flood tide eastwards. There are good cycle tracks and quiet lanes, and small, sandy beaches among the rocks.

NAVIGATION

Unless the heavy fogs have descended, as they often do on this coast, it's quite difficult to get lost. The impressive 84m (276ft)-high Île Vierge lighthouse to the north is unmissable (392 steps to the top), and although the Libenter buoy can be elusive, once you find it the rocky entrance starts to make sense and you are soon in sheltered water, with the Atlantic swell behind you. A marina was built in 2007, although some swinging moorings remain. In high season, you will often be met and given berthing directions.

OVERVIEW

L'Aber Wrac'h itself is hardly large enough to be called a village. You'll find it has a pleasant waterfront with cafés

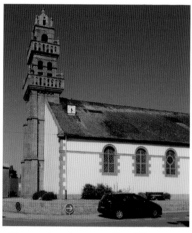

▲ The church at the centre of Landéda is a good landmark to aim for if walking

and bars, but for decent shopping you'll need to climb the hill to the village of Landéda (25 min walk).

There are conflicting theories about how the place got its name. Some say it is named after the first rock you come to in the approaches, 'Ar Gwrach', which means 'old woman'. Or it might be a name derived from the 'estuary of the fairy'.

The 'abers', or rias, define the nature of this part of Brittany, allowing the sea to reach deep into the countryside. This is the longest and most northerly of the Brittany rias. There is now a growing kelp production industry, the harvesting taking place between May and October. They call kelp 'Brittany's black gold'; it's used in shampoo, toothpaste, salad dressings and cakes.

THINGS TO SEE AND DO

Aber Wrac'h Diving, on the harbour, offers training courses up to Level 3. Ask at the harbour office for kayaking, paddle boarding, diving and sea fishing. This is the place for all kinds of watersports and tuition.

There is a good coastal hiking route westwards from the harbour before turning northwards to Pen Nez, then doubling back towards the marina (10.5km/6.5 miles), described as 'moderate' walking.

Visits can be arranged to the Île Vierge lighthouse. Consult the tourist information office close by the marina.

The essentials:

FUEL On the marina (credit card).

CHANDLERY Comptoir de la Mer, on the harbour with an excellent range of fishing tackle.

REPAIRS Agence Technique Marine Plaisance, to be found a short walk to the east of the marina is offering repairs, engine parts and overwintering.

LAUNDRY On the marina, and also in the supermarket at Landéda (see photo on page 18).

HIRE Cycle hire at 41 Ar Palud, close to the harbour, but check with the harbour office.

▼ Close by the marina, safe and sheltered sailing for all ages

Fast ferries to the lighthouse leave from Kastell Ac'h (30 min by taxi).

FOOD AND SHOPPING

- Bread from the **Café du Port**.
- **Supermarché Utile**, 9 Place de l'Europe, Landéda (25 min walk). There is a bus service to Landéda from outside the Café du Port.

- For stocking up, **Lanilis** has several supermarkets including Aldi (10 min by taxi).

FURTHER AFIELD

Buses to Brest (Bus No 20, 35 min) from the Café du Port, which allows for crew changes via the airport at Brest. If no flights, then the TGV runs from Brest to Paris via Morlaix, from where you can catch a bus or train to Roscoff and take a ferry to Plymouth from there.

Tourist information
Large black building by the harbour car park.

▼ The nearby small town of Landéda is best for provisions

▼ Roscoff – don't be put off by the drying harbour.
A large marina with all weather access is close by

ROSCOFF/BLOSCON

FALMOUTH 95NM, **TRÉBEURDEN** 25NM, **L'ABER WRAC'H** 30NM,
GUERNSEY 70NM

The old harbour at Roscoff dries, which once made it less attractive as a destination. Now there is a marina – not in the old harbour but round the corner in what is Port Bloscon, where the Plymouth ferries arrive. It's a small town but bursting with character and known for the mildness of its climate.

It's a 25 min walk from the marina into the old town centre. There's a shuttle from the marina to the old harbour in July and August.

NAVIGATION

This is a very convenient marina at the western end of the Channel and available in all weathers and at all states on tide. Because of the open-ended nature of the breakwater, the tide flows swiftly through parts of the marina, especially in the vicinity of the hammerheads. When entering, take the northern entrance.

There is only one walkway from the marina to the shore, and if you're looking for the nearest toilets, it's the grey block, afloat, on the westermost pontoon. Look out for a blue RIB on arrival and they will point you to a berth. Full facilities ashore.

OVERVIEW

In the 19th century locals exported onions from here in large quantities, making this the home of the 'Onion Johnnies', who travelled to England on bicycles, the handlebars laden with Roscoff pink onions. More than a thousand 'Johnnies' a year came over to England during the 1920s.

The merchants of Roscoff once also traded in cloth, salt and wood. Everything about the place looks seaward for inspiration, with sculptures of boats carved out of stone, and a maze of cellars, once the lairs of pirates.

Roscoff is now a major production centre for seaweed. Because of the supposed curative powers of the local

▲ This is home of the Onion Johnnies so expect onions to be much in evidence

sea water, in 1899 a Dr Bagot came here and established the first thalassotherapy (sea water therapy) centre.

You'll enjoy the 16th-century granite buildings, and even more the vast range of seafood the restaurants and cafés serve here.

The marina was completed in 2016. It's far less atmospheric than the old harbour, but it's a lot less hassle when the tide goes out.

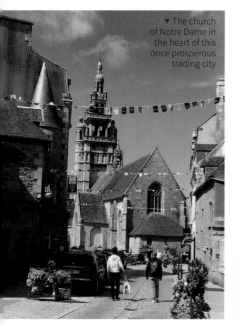

▼ The church of Notre Dame in the heart of this once prosperous trading city

The essentials:

FUEL By credit card from the fuel berth under the harbour wall.

REPAIRS Large Travelift and chandlery on the marina – Comptoir de la Mer.

FACILITIES Afloat on the marina – small grey building (swipe card needed) – and also ashore close to the harbour office – a lengthy glass structure. All facilities reported to be top class.

LAUNDRY On the marina.

THINGS TO SEE AND DO

Visit **Onion Johnny Museum**, 48 rue Brizeux (10 min walk), preferably with a beret on the head and a cigarette on the lips. The life and times of the Onion Johnnies are celebrated here. Pink onion tastings are also on offer.

The **Île de Batz** lies only 15 min by ferry from Roscoff. It's a place to sample the quiet and unhurried face of Brittany as enjoyed by its 800 inhabitants. The harbour is shallow and dries to hard sand. For a relaxed day out, a ferry out to Île de Batz might be a good idea. By not taking your own boat, though, you would miss the peace that descends once the tourists have left for the night.

FOOD AND SHOPPING

● Like the famous rosé wines, the Roscoff onions have a similar pinkish hue and have been grown here since the 17th century. There is an **Onion Festival** in August. Make sure to take some on board. Remember the wise words of explorer and high latitudes sailor, Bill Tilman, who said 'never board a ship without an onion'.
● Some **provisions on the marina** (croissants can be ordered the previous night).
● **Epicerie Roscoff**, 9 rue Gambetta, 20 min walk.
● **Market day** is Wednesday.

▲ Roscoff is officially described as 'a small town of Breton character'

FURTHER AFIELD

Being a ferry port (Brittany Ferries to Plymouth) connections from here are good. Trains to Morliax (40 min roughly every two hours) or Bus 29 takes you to Morlaix or Brest. Buses can be found outside the ferry terminal.

There is a regular ferry service between Plymouth and Roscoff (Brittany Ferries) and seasonal services between Roscoff and Bilbao (Spain) and Cork (Ireland).

Tourist information
Quai d'Auxerre, 20 min walk

MORLAIX

TRÉBEURDEN 23NM, **ROSCOFF** 9NM, **LÉZARDRIEUX** 60NM, **CHENAL DU FOUR** 55NM

There are winding streets in the old quarter of town, and plenty of well-preserved medieval buildings, said to be some of the best in Brittany. The marina has a workmanlike, rather than a touristic atmosphere. It's nearly 16km (10 miles) from the sea, so there's perfect shelter and it's a safe place to leave a boat.

NAVIGATION

It is a well-marked river but don't attempt to cut corners, and make sure to avoid the mid-channel Château du Taureau, built in the 16th century to keep the English out. It's a very attractive river for much of its length. You'll know when you're approaching the town by the sight of the towering granite viaduct – not to be confused with a routine, modern concrete bridge further downstream. If you are early for the lock you can lie to the quay on the approach. Careful when jumping on to the pontoons – they wobble. You'll find that the marina is pretty much in the centre of town, with a harbourmaster who will often help with your lines.

OVERVIEW

The greatest period of prosperity for Morlaix was in the 16th century when it was a thriving trading port and helped to make Brittany an important maritime power. It is also a place of

art and history. Many of the substantial houses were built by prosperous merchants, and hints of the wealth can still be seen in the harbour area. Some of the larger houses have been redeveloped as arts centres so expect to find all manner of performance and exhibitions to entertain you.

Although welcome today, English sailors were not greeted with open arms in 1522 when a fleet sailed upriver, knowing the French army was away at the time and the merchants were at a local fair. The English wore disguises and burned and pillaged the entire town, removing much wine to their boats. This was their downfall because having drunk themselves to oblivion, they were in no state to fight off the returning French army and were all slaughtered. That's how the mid-river

château came to be built – to keep the English out. The Morlaix town motto, 'If they bite you, bite them back', is said to date from that time.

▼ Once you see the viaduct (which carries the TGV to Paris) you're almost there

THINGS TO SEE AND DO

Duchess Anne's House 33 rue du Mur, (20 min walk) is said to be the oldest in town and is now a museum. It dates from the Renaissance and is famed for its covered interior courtyard, or lantern, complete with huge fireplace – this style of building is unique to Morlaix. Look hard at the timber exterior to spot the intricate sculptures, many of them saints.

The **Museum of the Jacobins**, Place de Jacobins (20 min walk) is a former 13th-century convent and is now the municipal museum. There is modern art, traditional arts and crafts, and maritime heritage.

Take time to feed and water yourself at the **Café de la Terrasse**, 31 Place des Otages, no ordinary brasserie. It was established in 1872 around a central spiral staircase and is full of locals and rich on atmosphere.

▼ Fine medieval buildings in the backstreets of Morlaix

Although a good way out of town to the north, **Cairn de Barnenez** (20 min by taxi from town) is well worth a trip if you have a taste for ancient monuments. This is said to be the 'oldest building in the world' and dates from megalithic times, 5,000 years ago. It has been nicknamed the 'Prehistoric Parthenon'. You can't go in, but you can go round it and sense the ancient history. It sits on the Kernéléhen peninsula, which you will have passed on your port side as you headed from seaward towards the river.

FOOD AND SHOPPING

● Head south from the marina towards town, aiming to pass under the viaduct, and you'll see plentiful food shopping along the way including a **butchers** and **bakery**.
● For stocking up try **Intermarché**, 17 rue Jean Jaurès (25 min walk).
● The **local ales** come in black, brown or blonde and are highly recommended, in particular Coreff.
● This region is also famous for **artichokes** and **cauliflowers**.
● **Market day** is Saturday, and there is a food market beyond an antique market at **Place Allende** (20 min walk).

FURTHER AFIELD

The SNCF station (white building) is on the TGV line from Paris to Brest and is high up at the western end of the viaduct. There are train connections to Roscoff (35 min), which are useful for crew arrival/departures. Roscoff is only 30km (18.6 miles) away by road.

Gare de Morlaix, Place Rol Tanguy, is 10 min by taxi. The No 29 bus runs between Morlaix and Roscoff – the bus terminal is at the Gare de Morlaix.

Tourist information
10 Place Charles-De-Gaulle
(10 min walk)

TRÉBEURDEN

ROSCOFF 16NM, **MORLAIX** 22NM, **PLYMOUTH** 95NM, **JERSEY** 65NM

This hugely popular resort stands at the western end of Brittany's legendary pink granite coast. There's a top-class beach, excellent marina, and every imaginable watersport in a stunning Brittany setting. Less of a town, more a village, and a stiff uphill walk from the marina.

NAVIGATION

This is a useful coastal marina that can be open seven hours per tide, or even longer. The approach dries but is well marked and lit at night. There is a floodlit tide gauge on the sill and if the green light shows, there is 1.6m (5.25ft) over it. As with all these Brittany harbours that are contained by a sill, careful attention to the tidetables will ensure a happy ship.

▼ Splendid beach close by the marina

The essentials:

FUEL On the marina – good fuel dock on the harbour wall opposite the visitor pontoon (not 24 hr).

REPAIRS Contact ABC marine, who are 7 min away by car but will come to yachts on the marina.

LAUNDRY Behind the chandlery, Cap Marine, which is in the marina buildings.

HIRE Free e-bikes from the harbour office. Car hire is available in Lannion and they will come and collect you – the harbour office will arrange. There is a free summer shuttle bus service from the marina to the town centre; sometimes provided by an estate car. If they're not too busy, they'll drop you elsewhere within reason, even as far as Lannion.

OVERVIEW

If you want a good family beach holiday, this place takes some beating. There is also a rich variety of landscapes hereabouts with moorland, forest and salt marsh, much of which can be reached by walking the footpath GR 34. Standing stones and ancient tombs speak of human habitation here 20,000 years ago.

Brittany was a popular landing place for Welsh monks, and there is a strong religious tradition here, with many churches and chapels. The Chapel Penvern is one of the oldest in Brittany.

Beware the so-called Korrigans, the fairy folk – thumb-sized night-time spirits with pointed ears, beards and hooves who dance round fires. They hate religion, which is why they are so naughty and cross.

The Korrigans apart, Trébeurden has a family-friendly reputation. It's a ten-minute walk uphill to the town.

THINGS TO SEE AND DO

There are said to be six beaches but the principal two are separated by the peninsula of **Le Castel**, the more popular is **Plage de Tresmeur**, south from the marina (2 min walk).

Originally founded in 1300, **Chapel Penvern**, 21 rue de Keralegan (1 hr walk) is one of the oldest churches in the region, rebuilt in the 17th and 19th centuries. There are guided tours the first Saturday of each month.

Planétarium de Bretagne, route du Radôme, (10 min by taxi) is one of the largest planetariums in Europe, with daily shows for all ages starting as young as three. It includes a history

of space flights, a tour round the starry skies and lots of activities.

Village Gaulois is very close to the planetarium (above). This 'theme park' has lots for kids to do and raises money for villages in Africa. It has high-tech and free mechanical and hand-made games, zip wires and a hand-powered merry-go-round. The entrance fee is less than 10 euros and the crêpes are said to be world class. No child has emerged from this place unhappy.

FOOD AND SHOPPING

- **Bread** from the harbour office from 0800.
- **Groceries** on the marina in high season.
- **Shops** in the town may be closed on Wednesdays.
- For **basic shopping**, head towards the Place

▲ Trébeurden is a small town, much geared towards tourists

◀ A tidal marina protected by a sill, large and with all facilities

▶ All kinds of food at the extensive Tuesday market

de Crec H Héry, where you will find, apart from the tourist information, a bakery, small fruit and veg shop, pharmacy and butcher.

- **Intermarché SUPER Trébeurden et Drive**, 50 Rue des Plages, – take a taxi (5 min walk).
- There is a **food market** on Tuesday morning that also features **local craftsmen**, including sculptors, wood carvers and potters. Food market again on Saturday mornings, with a Friday market of local produce in high season.

FURTHER AFIELD

Buses to Lannion with connections to Morlaix. Trains from Morlaix to the Roscoff ferry.

Tourist information
Place de Crec H Héry (15 min walk)

CÔTE DE GRANIT ROSE
(THE PINK GRANITE COAST)
PERROS-GUIREC
▶ PAIMPOL

THE WIND AND THE WAVES may have carved the rocks along this coastline into the most fantastical shapes, but they can't wash the colour out of them. Look at the rocks long enough and you'll see one that looks like a bull's head, or is it a horse? Sometimes, they might even look like someone you know.

▼ Pink granite rocks and cliffs define this stretch of coastline

But it's their colour that will grab your eyes, every bit as much as their shape – the rocks are pink, and in the evening sun they simply glow. Once you move inland, the colour seems to go and you are left with ordinary, glum-looking grey stone, so the coast is simply the best place to be. Fingers of pink granite point out to sea, between them often secret beaches of fine, white sand, some sheltered by pines. The sea will be turquoise and you'll want to be in it.

If you want a break from sailing, this is a good stretch of coastline on which to pause a cruise. Get the boat settled in Trébeurden and set your sights on the 'customs officers' path' GR 34.

This stretch of coast is a great place to turn your back on the sea for a while and take the 11km (7 mile) river trip up to Tréguier to what they call the 'picture perfect town', with its narrow streets and medieval houses – a real taste of inland Brittany. A boat trip from Perros to Sept-Îsles, a national nature reserve, rewards you with puffins, gannets and cormorants.

The local speciality is mussels cooked in crème fraîche and lardons, and doubtless with garlic as well. There are other ways to enjoy mussels: steamed in white wine with shallots is traditional and, of course, chips on the side. But try moules à la Normande, cooked in a creamy sauce of white wine or local cider. You haven't tried the cider yet?

It is not possible to cruise this coast without enjoying the famous galettes, which are buckwheat 'pancakes' filled with ham, cheese or vegetables. If they're made with plain flour they're usually called crêpes and served sweet with butter, jam, honey and cream. If you see someone selling a galette wrapped tightly round a rich pork sausage, go for it!

PERROS-GUIREC

TRÉGUIER 20NM, **MORLAIX** 28NM, **L'ABER WRAC'H** 60NM, **FALMOUTH** 100NM

This is one of the most popular resorts in Brittany, fringed with the famous pink granite and two fine sand beaches. There is good surfing and walking on the coastline. The locals call it, simply, Perros. Expect it to be packed in high season. The town has won awards for its family-friendly nature.

NAVIGATION

It's a lengthy approach over drying sand and you must make careful calculations to ensure you can cross the sill. Signs warn of strong currents when the tide starts to overtop the sill. The entrance is narrow – 5.8m (19ft) – and you might think, at first glance, you are heading the wrong way.

OVERVIEW

There was once a granite mining industry here, from where rock was sent to Paris and used in some of the most imposing buildings.

There are really two towns: Perros Harbour and Perros Town. You can find a decent selection of shops and bars by the harbour, but the best is up the hill towards the main town. This is a spread-out kind of place with a bit of a routine feel to it, although pleasant enough. You'll be able to buy anything you seek, from high fashion to tea bags. Don't be surprised to see palm trees lining some of the streets thanks to this part of Brittany's temperate climate.

▼ A substantial marina contained by a sill

▲ An imposing harbour office on the shore, easily missed

The essentials:

FUEL Berth close to the lock.

REPAIRS Chandlery close to the marina, slipways and cranes for lifting. No major repairs.

FACILITIES Behind the capitainerie. Shared facilities for men and women, toilets in a separate area. If you can't get water in the shower, wave your hand to activate the motion sensor. Also at the yacht club at the top of the fuel pontoon.

LAUNDRY On the marina, or Laverie Automatique, 3 blvd. Jean Mermoz (25 min walk).

HIRE Electric bikes available for hire from the capitainerie.

Much of the best action in terms of beaches and town shopping might mean half an hour's walking, although in high season there is a bus service.

THINGS TO SEE AND DO

Plage de Trestraou (30 min walk) is the main beach, long and sandy with a promenade behind the beach. **Plage de Trestrignel** (35 min walk) is smaller but more attractive and set among rocky headlands. There is a huge range of beach activities so children won't get bored – from beach clubs, to miniature golf, a skate park, diving and kayaking.

Sept-Îles consists of seven islands and is a must for bird lovers – you may see puffins, fulmars, kittiwakes, gannets (20,000 pairs) and Manx shearwaters. Boat trips from **Perros-Guirec** with Armor, blvd. Joseph le Bihan (35 min walk, close to Plage de Trestaou) take about 2 hr. Monks tried to build monasteries here, but gave up – it's that kind of wild, rocky place but if you're lucky you might land.

FOOD AND SHOPPING

● **Le Relais du Port**, 45 rue Anatole le Braz (3 min walk) is the closest supermarket (if a little modest), but there are many shops on the waterfront selling wine, bread and fish.
● **Carrefour City**, 2 blvd. Aristide Briand (20 min uphill walk north from the marina).
● **Market day** is Friday with a small market near the marina on Wednesday.
● **Shops** are often closed on Sunday and Monday.

FURTHER AFIELD

The nearest SNCF station is at Lannion (Brest–Paris line) (20 min by taxi).

Tourist information
21 Place de l'Hôtel de Ville
(20 min walk)

TRÉGUIER

ST HELIER 53NM, **GUERNSEY** 50NM, **PAIMPOL** 20NM, **ROSCOFF** 40NM,
PLYMOUTH 95NM

This is an all-weather harbour and small medieval town 11km (7 miles) from the sea along the picturesque Jaundy River. There are good anchorages along the way. A short (uphill) walk from the marina takes you to a little jewel of a place with beguiling 15th- and 16th-century timbered houses, 'a picture-perfect town'.

NAVIGATION

Day or night, whatever the weather, the river mouth is safe to approach. There are plenty of lighthouses for reassurance. Good buoyage as far as the marina. A mid-river waiting pontoon allows you to choose to enter the marina at slack water, which is recommended.

There is quite a strong cross tide (up to 9 knots reported) running through the pontoons at anything other than slack water, so moor with care.

OVERVIEW

The town was founded in the 6th century on the site of a monastery found by St Tudwal, who had Welsh origins, and was one of the seven founder saints of Brittany. The *Tro Breizh* is a tour of Brittany; it passes through the seven towns, Tréguier included. Interestingly, at the time of Tudwal (Tugdual in French) the Welsh language was understood by Breton speakers. The cathedral in Tréguier is dedicated to him and given the small size of the town, to have its own cathedral seems rather grand.

▼ Half-timbered houses, now galleries and bookshops

▲ Uphill walk from the marina to a wide choice of eating and drinking

The essentials:

FUEL On the north side of E pontoon, but only attempt at slack water.

REPAIRS Nearby boatyard has a 20T boatlift, and crane. Most repairs can be undertaken here.

FACILITIES All facilities at the harbour office and, unusually, there are reports that the Wi-Fi actually works as far out as the visitor pontoons. The harbour office is up the stairs; everything else, including a bar, is on the ground floor.

LAUNDRY Available on the marina.

CAR HIRE Can be arranged through the marina office. Garage Bodson (Renault dealer) will collect you from the harbour office, otherwise it's a 35 min walk to their showroom.

However, it is more a reflection of the scale of the pilgrimages here to celebrate Tudwal. There is no longer a bishop's seat here, but the church is now given the courtesy title of 'cathedral'. St Ivo (or Yves) is also celebrated here as the patron saint of Brittany lawyers, and he is remembered in the town on his feast day, 19 May.

There is more culture evident here than in many Breton towns. Expect to find art galleries and second-hand bookshops. French writers have described the place as 'a jewel', with narrow streets and houses with internal gardens, glimpsed as you pass by.

THINGS TO SEE AND DO

Cathédrale St-Tugdual, 1 Place du Général Leclerc (12 min walk) is the former cathedral of the town. It has three towers from different periods. The 18th-century tower was financed

▼ A good marina, best entered or left at slack water. Walkways can be steep at LW

by Louis XVI having won the Paris lottery, hence the unusual holes, which are shaped like playing cards. Who said gambling never pays off? This is one of the greatest churches in Brittany with breathtaking glasswork and stalls dating from the Renaissance. A coffee stop in the cathedral square comes highly recommended.

There is good walking on the **GR 34**, the old customs officers' path, which will take you round the headland to **Port Blanc**.

FOOD AND SHOPPING
- **Votre Marché**, 6 blvd. Anatole le Braz (15 min walk).
- **Super U et Drive**, 4 blvd. Jean Guéhenno (25 min walk).
- **Bio coop Lunesol Tréguier** (organic food shop), rue Marcellin Berthelot (2 min walk).
- There is a **farmers' market** on Wednesdays, sometimes stretching from close to the marina as far as the cathedral.

FURTHER AFIELD
Buses leave/arrive at the High School Joseph Savina, rue de la République (20 min walk). Buses to St Brieuc and high-speed rail connections from there to Paris with changes to all major ferry ports in Brittany.

Tourist information
In the same building as the harbour office

▼ A grand cathedral for quite a small town

LÉZARDRIEUX

TRÉGUIER 25NM, **GUERNSEY** 45NM, **JERSEY** 45NM, **ALDERNEY** 65NM, **TORQUAY** 100NM

This is a quiet place on the western bank of the Trieux River and a pleasant 6NM trip upriver from Île de Bréhat. South of Lézardrieux is a high-level bridge (17m/56ft clearance but check) and if you can scrape under there is the possibility of making for Portrieux, a town described as the 'little Venice' of the region, a further 7NM inland.

NAVIGATION

You can enter the river in all weathers and at all states of tide. Be aware that the tides run hard in this river, and anchoring space is limited by permanent moorings. Even in the outer parts of the marina, particularly on the hammerheads, the cross tide setting through the marina can be

▲ This is a maintenance depot for the local buoys and lighthouses. It is the old optic from the Triagoz light (1925–1981)

troublesome. The marina has 50 visitor berths. The harbour staff here are less attentive than in some of the nearby resorts – don't expect to be met by a launch. It's a help yourself kind of place.

OVERVIEW

Lézardrieux, with a population of only 600 people, is far less a resort than many of its glossier neighbours, so expect the choice of shops and restaurants to be limited. The town is 1.6km (1 mile) uphill walk from the marina. This village lies on the eastern side of what has become known as the Lézardrieux

The essentials: ⚓

FUEL On the marina – landward end of the first pontoon you come to on arrival.

REPAIRS Gourenez Nautic – all marine services on the harbour. The boatyard has 50T lifting facilities and all engineering services.

LAUNDRY Laverie du Port, 67 rue du Port (2 min walk).

HIRE Electric bikes are available at the harbour office.

▼ Lézardrieux town is small, but friendly, and sits at the top of the hill above the river. It's uphill for shopping

peninsula with good, peaceful, walking. The meeting of the sea waters of the Channel, and the fresher river water, creates rich grounds for a variety of wildlife.

FOOD AND SHOPPING

- **Utile Supermarché U**, 9 rue du 8 Mai (10 min walk).
- **Boulangerie du Centre**, 26 Place du Centre (7 min walk).
- **Market day** is Friday.

FURTHER AFIELD

Nearest train station at Paimpol (with connections to the Brest–Paris TGV line) with bus connection (BreizhGo) to Lézardrieux. Bus station at rue de l'Hermitage (15 min walk), close to the supermarché.

Tourist information
Place du Centre (7 min walk)

PAIMPOL

ST QUAY PORTRIEUX 11NM, **GUERNSEY** 45NM, **SALCOMBE** 90NM, **ROSCOFF** 45NM

This is a granite-faced, typical Breton harbour. Cobbled alleyways make for a compact, enjoyable and safe harbour if you are brave or experienced enough to attempt the many twists and turns over drying sand, which you must cross to get to the place. There's quite a smart feel here.

NAVIGATION

There are two marinas and the capitainerie can be found on the dividing wall between them. One lock gives access to both and the lock operates free-flow roughly 1 hr before HW. Expect to raft in high season. Bassin No 1 is to the east, Bassin No 2 to the west. Berths are close together.

OVERVIEW

The cod and whale hunters sailed from here in the 19th century, setting off in February and not returning until September, making for a town that was largely deserted in the summer. The coastline grows harsher hereabouts and the place has a feeling of wildness about it. The town is famous for its oysters, but all kinds of fish to be had are in abundance ashore. The town can become very crowded in the high season. Some will come here just for sea air and the shopping.

THINGS TO SEE AND DO

If you time your visit for the first weekend in August, enjoy the **Festival du Chant de Marin** – sea shanties – and the gathering of traditional craft. The **Latin Quarter** is a maze of narrow streets leading to the fishing harbour. The **Musée de la Mer**, the maritime museum, rue de Labenne (10 min walk from the marina) is housed in a former cod-drying shed. There's lots of explanation of the traditional fishing and shipbuilding here.

▼ There's a strong Breton feel to this town, with back streets to wander

A vintage train line, **La Vapeur du Trieux**, does trips between Paimpol and St Quay Portrieux – see vapeurdutrieux. com for the timetable. It's a treat.

The best beaches to be found in Brittany are not here, but try **Plage de la Tossen**, which you can find by walking east from the harbour. There's also a sea-water swimming pool.

Ferries from the harbour (subject to tide) to Île de Bréhat (10 min walk). Good walking and hiking on the nearby **GR 34**.

FOOD AND SHOPPING

● **Boulangerie Le Fournil du Port**, 49 ave. Maurice Thorez, on the south side of Bassin No 1, and others within the town.
● **Carrefour** (hypermarket), rue Raymond Pellier (20 min walk).
● **Carrefour City**, 11 rue St-Vincent (5 min walk).
● **Market day** is Tuesday, with occasional evening markets.
● Look out for the **coco de Paimpol** – this looks like a haricot bean with a nutty and flowery flavour. Top-class in stews and soups and only found in this region.

FURTHER AFIELD

● Trains from **Paimpol station**, 22 Av. du Général de Gaulle, take you to Guingamp (six trains a day), from where you can get connections to
● Paris, Brest or Rennes, which has some flights to the UK.

The essentials:

FUEL On the marina, on the quay.

REPAIRS All kinds of maintenance needs by consulting the harbour office.

CHANDLERY Dauphin Nautic, Quai Armand Dayot, on the eastern side of the harbour not far from the lock (10 min walk).

Île de Brehat

There is no easy anchorage here, no water at LW and no facilities, so if you find yourself in Paimpol waiting for weather, this will make for a good day out.

This is one of the most atmospheric islands off the Brittany coast, packed with tourists in the summer but still worth a visit. There are no cars on the island. The vegetation is rich and the variety of flowers is legendary thanks to the microclimate. There is also a colony of 250 puffins, some excellent hiking, cycling and even fine dining as well as the usual tourist fare. Look out for an organic farm, which bakes bread daily.

There is only one ferry service, Les Vedettes de Bréhat, and their service runs year-round from Pointe de l'Arcouest, which can be found to the north of Paimpol (10 min ferry ride).

Tourist information

Place de la République (5 min walk)

◀ 1 A welcome sight if you have children on board; 2 Boats of all kinds are welcome here; 3 Plenty of back streets to wander; 4 It's a compact harbour but safe and secure; 5 There's a rich variety of shopping experiences – and galleries for those with deeper pockets

CÔTE D'ÉMERAUDE

(THE EMERALD COAST, INCLUDING BAIE DE ST BRIEUC)

ST QUAY PORTRIEUX ▶ ST MALO

▼ The lighthouse of Cap Fréhel stands guard over the emerald coast of Brittany

THIS COAST GETS ITS NAME from the colour of the sea. Cap Fréhel with its 70m (230ft)-high cliffs is the defining headland on this stretch of coastline, between the two very attractive harbours of St Quay Portrieux and St Malo.

No trip to Brittany is complete without a couple of days in St Malo, walking the ramparts and enjoying the vast range of high-quality food on offer. St Cast le Guildo and Binic offer good marinas, close to fine sandy beaches, and if you have children on board all these resorts will keep them occupied on the dreariest of days.

Swimming pools that capture the tide are a feature here and provide bathing opportunities when the tide has retreated almost to the horizon. They are very safe with no flow of tide. There's one in St Malo and at Binic.

Enjoy the history, which includes prehistoric remains and forts from a multitude of wars. On the beaches, wait for the tide to ebb and paddle around on the rock pools.

In the bay off St Brieuc (nearest harbour Binic) taste the scallops. They have been harvesting them here since the Middle Ages. These days they dredge 6,500T a year and if that sounds a lot, be assured the fishing is tightly regulated. The season runs from 1 October to 15 May. They celebrate the scallop in Paimpol and St Quay Portrieux every year in April in a major two-day scallop-consuming festival.

Have you come across Far Breton yet? It can be eaten as a cake or a pudding. It's a kind of custardy flan jewelled with prunes and raisins which may, or may not, have been soaked in alcohol. Traditionally, it is baked until almost black – quite delicious, and keeps for days on a boat, if you can resist it.

ST QUAY PORTRIEUX

ST HELIER 40NM, ST MALO 35NM, TRÉBEURDEN 30NM, PLYMOUTH 115NM

This town is a smart place these days but an old-fashioned resort at heart. You'll find horse riding, tennis, golf and a casino, and a choice of beaches in the shelter of a rocky coastline.

NAVIGATION

This stretch of coast is guarded by a long, rocky reef to the NE, which requires careful navigation. There are 100 visitor berths with all-tide, all-weather access making it useful for a first landing if crossing the Channel.

It is the biggest deep-water marina in Brittany and was opened by the legendary French yachtsman Éric Tabarly in 1990.

OVERVIEW

This was a fishing port in the 18th century engaged in the Newfoundland trade, but a resort in the 19th century. Although some of the narrow back streets and closely packed houses by the old drying harbour can still be seen, the waterfront is now eclipsed by the substantial marina, which

▼ …but a far better and busier one on the far side of the marina. Walk to the island at low water (LW)

The essentials:

FUEL Self-service 24/7 with credit card payment.

CHANDLERY Cooperative Maritime on the walk from the marina into town.

REPAIRS The marina can advise on repairs. There is a choice of electronic and mechanical engineers, and a boatyard.

FACILITIES Toilets 24 hr with code or card key access.

LAUNDRY On the marina.

HIRE Cycle hire from the marina office. Also, car hire and taxis and advice on delivery options for provisions, making this an ideal place to restock after a cross-Channel trip and before heading for the more remote harbours and anchorages.

▼ A modest beach fronts the town (no swimming allowed)...

detracts from what was once a typical Breton fishing community. Outside the summer sailing months, this place is at its busiest when shellfish, sea bass and mackerel are the major catches.

THINGS TO SEE AND DO

The **beaches** here are good, and two are close by the marina. Because of unusual crystals in the sand here, you can watch the beaches alter colour with the tide and changing sunlight. **Plage du Casino** has a sea-water swimming pool (20 min walk north of Pointe du Sémaphore). This is usually the busiest beach. **Plage du Châtelet** is to the north of Pointe du Sémaphore, behind the casino's pool, and is free for public use. **Plage de la Comtesse** is also to the north of the marina. A good family beach with views to La Comtesse. Lifeguards in season. Walk to the island at low tide. Showers, toilets and a host of cafés. Also a merry-go-round. **Portrieux beach** is a short walk from the marina at the head of the old drying harbour. It is less popular and there's no swimming allowed.

FOOD AND SHOPPING

● **Votre Marché**, 50 Quai de la République (6 min walk on the far side of the old harbour). Will deliver to boats.

▼ It's a town that likes to dress itself up

▼ This is one of those massive Breton marinas. Expect your sailing holiday to turn into a walking holiday if you're unlucky with your berth

- **Spar**, 4 rue Jeanne d'Arc (20 min walk).
- **Le Fournil du Port** (bakery), 1 rue du Commerce (6 min walk).
- **Market day** is Monday in the old port, and Friday morning in the town.
- Scallops are the most famous dish round here so don't miss a chance to try **Coquille St Jacques**.
- There's a **scallop festival** in late April, but only every three years so you might be unlucky.

FURTHER AFIELD

- The nearest station is **Gare St Brieuc**, 22000 Saint-Brieuc, with TGV connections. Tickets can be bought at the tourist information. There are bus connections to St Brieuc with the TIBUS network, and from there onward connections to Brest with an airport for a crew change.

Tourist information
17 bis rue Jeanne-d'Arc (20 min walk) northwards. Look out for the Stella Maris College and the period roundabout opposite with galloping horses

▼ Eating and drinking opportunities overlooking the marina

BINIC

This is a very friendly seaside resort with a clean and tidy marina, and plenty of shops, cafés and bistros along the waterfront. There is close access to the beach, and a sea-water swimming pool by the side of the marina. If you have children to entertain, this is the place to head for. It has been described as a romantic place – so there's something for everyone.

NAVIGATION

It's an easy approach but it dries. Towards HW you'll find 3m (10ft) over the sill controlled by traffic lights. Very good shelter here with any W in the wind. If early on the tide, you could anchor off and wait.

OVERVIEW

Once a fishing harbour with Newfoundland cod connections, this was an important fishing centre, hence the wealthy, granite-faced shipowners' houses. Walk the Quai Jean Bart to get an impression of how important this harbour once was. It is now given over entirely to pleasure, and plenty of it. The relaxed atmosphere is helped by the rolling green fields that back on to the town.

THINGS TO SEE AND DO

There are two beaches to choose from. **Plage de la Banche** is just to the south of the marina with a sandy beach but where the tide goes out a long way – great for families. To the north, the

They talk of a sense of romance in Binic

▲ Very good shelter in the marina, top left

The essentials:

FUEL None at the marina but available in cans onshore.

REPAIRS Ask at the capitainerie for electronic and engine repairs.

CHANDLERY Marinocéan, 6 ave. Foch (10 min walk at the far end of the marina) – electronics, chandlery, clothing etc.

FACILITIES Good showers and toilets at the capitainerie to starboard, just after you enter the marina.

LAUNDRY Laverie Binic Allée des Prés Verts (25 min walk to northern outskirts of town).

Plage de l'Avant Port is more secluded and less used than Plage de la Blance, and a short walk from the capitainerie through the car park.

Musée d'Art et Traditions Populaires, 3 rue de l'Ic (10 min walk) houses popular art and traditions of Brittany, and is strong on maritime themes, the long-distance Canadian fisheries, and domestic history including agriculture and traditional crafts.

It is worth checking out **L'Estran cultural centre**, ave. Général de Gaulle (10 min walk) – a mixed space used for concerts, drama, etc.

Check out the dates of the Binic Cod Festival, **La P'tite Morue en Fête**. It's a traditional craft gathering with music and plenty of fish, usually held at the beginning of the summer.

The **Binic Folk Blues Festival** attracts big crowds. The stage is close to the marina, so be warned: it happens in late July – take note if you want to avoid it!

The **GR 34** threads its way through the town and along the coastline.

FOOD AND SHOPPING

● **Boulangerie Jacob Vincent**, 4 Place de l'Église (5 min walk) – bright red frontage.
● For **gourmet treats**, Samovar et Pain d'Épices, 24 rue Joffre (5 min walk).
● **Binic Eod Sarl**, 4 blvd. du Gén Leclerc (8 min walk).
● **Carrefour City**, 4 blvd. du Gén Leclerc (8 min walk).
● One of the largest **markets** in the region is held on Thursdays, with 200 vendors in the summer months along the quayside.

▲ The marina is protected by a sill. Anchor off if insufficient water

FURTHER AFIELD

Taxi to St Brieuc (15 min). Buses to St Brieuc (28 min) for further connections. The nearest train station is in St Brieuc, TGV connection to Paris (2 hr 17 min) or Brest (1 hr 35 min). Train to St Malo via Rennes from St Brieuc (for ferry and crew change) (2 hr).

Tourist information
6 Place Le Pomellec (10 min walk)

▼ Once inside, a safe and secure harbour close to the town

LE LÉGUÉ

▶ The most popular café is to be found in Plérin on the north side of the river

JERSEY 43NM, **GUERNSEY** 55NM, **ST QUAY PORTRIEUX** 11NM, **PLYMOUTH** 120NM

This is a workmanlike harbour with a canal-like feel at the mouth of the Gouët River and it serves as the harbour for the local capital, St Brieuc, to the south-west. Expect few leisure facilities, although things are improving. This is a good place for serious repairs if needed, or to leave a boat in complete safety.

NAVIGATION

Do not attempt in NE winds in excess of F5. The approach is lengthy and shallow. The basin is locked with traffic lights. Once through, proceed to Bassin No 2 via a swing bridge. The marina has had considerable upgrades in recent years to attract more passing trade, with new pontoons and a footbridge giving easy access to a new shower block and the small collection of shops and cafés. There are 20 visitor berths.

The Bureau de Port is on the south side of the river, just to seaward of the high bridge.

OVERVIEW

If you can imagine this place without its modern industrialisation and commercial activity, you see a rather attractive harbour in a wooded river valley. It still has its 18th-century ship chandlers' houses. Long-distance fishing, as far as Newfoundland, was conducted from here, and whaling. They once made spare parts for cars in factories along the river bank – the buildings are now a conference centre

▼ Everything here is overshadowed by the viaduct which carries the N12 trunk road

and restaurant. Building work is ongoing to create less industrial and more inviting surroundings.

THINGS TO SEE AND DO

Carré Rosengart, 16 Quai Armez, is a development on the south side of the marina in what was once the factory where the outboard motor was first developed. It now hosts exhibitions and marine activities, such as design and engineering workshops. Guided tours by arrangement with the tourist information (below).

If you are lucky, the *Grand Léjon* will be alongside – a two-masted sailing lugger, typical of these waters over a century ago and used for fishing and sand dredging.

Juno Bravo, 1 Quai Armez (on the marina) is a former RAF pinnace built in Cowes and in service until 1972. It now houses a museum of wooden toys.

FOOD AND SHOPPING

● **Bakery, coffee shops** and a **decent café** in the parade of shops on the north side of the river in the village of Plérin (on north bank of marina). Look for the village square for **bistros** and a **garage**.
● No supermarket in the village. **Carrefour Express**, 3 rue Houvenagle, and other good shopping, can be found in St Brieuc (30 min walk to the centre).

FURTHER AFIELD

Train station at St Brieuc, trains to Paris (2 hr 15 min), Rennes and Brest.

A summer shuttle bus operates from here to resorts Binic, Étables-sur-Mer, St Quay Portrieux. Bus R runs between Plérin and St Brieuc (departures every 30 min). Bus station in Plérin, Rond-Point de l'Europe 22190 (5 min walk).

The essentials:

FUEL None at the marina but there's a service station close by – look for the village square.

REPAIRS There is a ship repair facility that takes craft up to 350T, and you will be able to find all manner of expertise. Its paint shop has a good reputation. Yacht lift-out facilities with mast removal and large hard-standing area.

CHANDLERY In the Carré Rosengart shopping mall on the south bank, close by the Bureau du Port.

Tourist information
16 Quai Armez, part of Carré Rosengart

DAHOUËT

ST CAST 16NM, BINIC 10NM, ST MALO 28NM, GRANVILLE 45NM, GUERNSEY 50NM

Dahouët is a charming, almost hidden village among the rocks. There is little apparent tourist development, but there's good food here, and coastal walking. The friendly resort town of Pléneuf-Val-André is 30 min walk away with an excellent beach and good shopping.

NAVIGATION

The marina was built in 1989 with 36 visitor berths. The approach dries to 5m (16ft) and is protected by a sill. Deep draught vessels should calculate carefully at neap tides. The entrance is marked by red and green poles, and deeper water may be found to starboard. There is a tide gauge as you enter but this may cover at HW! Friendly, with a helpful harbourmaster.

The essentials:

FUEL No fuel on the marina.

REPAIRS There are no repair facilities, but this is a good place to dry out on a firm bottom for underwater work. Consult the harbour office. There is a chandlery on the north side of the harbour.

FACILITIES The showers and toilets are in the same block as the capitainerie – blue and white building. Also showers at the yacht club close to the visitor pontoons. Showers are free.

LAUNDRY None in the village. Lavomatique Pléneuf-Val-André, 18 Place de Lourmel (40 min walk).

◄ The waterside houses are as Breton as you can get

▶ **1** Once inside, you'll find a spacious and secure marina in the heart of the village; **2** The approach is between rocks but well marked; **3** Traditional classic, very much at home in this unspoilt setting – she's a reconstruction but available for tours; **4** It's a pleasant quayside to wander, with walks that take you easily to the coast; **5** The harbour opens out after a narrow, winding entrance

OVERVIEW

The 4th-century sailors of Dahouët were among the first to cross the Atlantic to Newfoundland to exploit the lucrative cod fishery. Later, the Vikings found the hidden nature of the harbour useful for their marauding activities.

THINGS TO SEE AND DO

The town of **Pléneuf-Val-André** is worth a visit, with a wide range of shopping, cafés and bars. The lengthy beach here is a major attraction and the area is popular with cliff-top walkers.

A reconstruction of an early 20th-century sailing ship, a fishing lugger, *La Pauline*, will take you on a short tour.

FOOD AND SHOPPING

● There is little shopping here apart from a **boulangerie** on the north side of the harbour and a handful of **bistros**.
● For the best shopping, walk to the town of **Pléneuf-Val-André** to the north-east (30 min).

▲ Watch the tide gauge on approach. The marina is protected by a sill

● **E Leclerc Hyper Pleneuf** (supermarket), 15 rue de St-Alban (35 min walk) – there is a bus to Pléneuf-Val-André in the summer months.

FURTHER AFIELD

Buses to St Briec (40 min) leave from the church in Pléneuf-Val-André. Nearest train station at Lamballe, 4 blvd. Jobert, (20 min by taxi).

> **Tourist information**
> In Pléneuf-Val-André, 1 rue Winston Churchill (30 min walk, near the seafront). SNCF rail tickets can be bought here

ST CAST
(ST CAST LE GUILDO)

ST MALO 12NM, **GUERNSEY** 50NM, **PAIMPOL** 30NM, **TORQUAY** 120NM

This is a stylish and tidy town, well groomed, and with a sweeping beach of soft white sand and a sparkling marina.

NAVIGATION

This is an easy marina to enter, and despite the considerable range of tides there is no sill or lock gates. Built within the last decade, it is smart, clean and offers all facilities. Red and green buoys mark the entrance channel. There are 40 visitor berths, swinging moorings also. Watch out for crab and lobster pots on the way in, and be aware that the walkways can be steep at low water. Showers have wet and dry areas, hairdryers and en suite hand washing. There are two washing machines and a sink for washing plates, saucepans etc (15 min walk into the centre of town).

OVERVIEW

Historically speaking, there's not a lot here for Brits to enjoy: in 1758, at the battle of St Cast, the English fleet, which had been prevented from taking the River Rance, was forced to retreat here. On landing, they came under ferocious assault from the French and 1,200 English sailors were lost.

▼ A wide, sandy beach both close to the town and the marina

▼ Packed in high season, but there are many shopping opportunities here

The essentials:

⚓

FUEL Diesel on the fishermen's pontoon, G.

REPAIRS Excellent facilities for boat lifting, mast removal etc. Small chandlery.

LAUNDRY On the marina or Ohier, 31 blvd. Duponchel (20 min walk).

HIRE Cycle hire at Vélo Aventure, 35 rue de la Résistance (10 min by taxi to the south of the town).

Founded by a Welsh monk, there remains a few of its old and narrow streets, but much of the development came from a rapid rise in the tourist industry in the 19th century when St Cast had a reputation as a chic resort, hence the substantial, posh villas.

THINGS TO SEE AND DO

Kids will love St Cast Aventure Chemin des Écureuils Le Bois Bras (15 min by taxi). Treetop adventures here are graded to suit all ages from 3+.

Walk north from the marina to enjoy the headland, with two further beaches round the corner. By taking the GR 34 coastal trail you can walk from here to St-Brieuc. Of course, you can enjoy this path without going all the way. Ask at the tourist information about guided shellfish picking walks – good for families.

FOOD AND SHOPPING

● Carrefour City, Place Charles-De-Gaulle (opposite tourist info) (20 min walk).
● Order croissants at the marina the night before.

● Market day is Monday during the summer months.
● Two cafés on the marina: Le Café Face and Caravel Coffee Café, both Résidence la Capitainerie

FURTHER AFIELD

Nearest train station at Lamballe (40 min by taxi), with a bus connection operated by SNCF. Three buses a day (Ti Bus) to St Malo (1 hr). Ferry connection. You can find the bus stop close to tourist information (see below).

Tourist information
Place Charles-De-Gaulle (20 min – opposite Carrefour City)

▼ It's a smart marina and, unusually for hereabouts, has no sill. Very helpful staff

ST MALO

JERSEY 30NM, **GUERNSEY** 50NM, **CHERBOURG** 80NM, **DARTMOUTH** 120NM

This is the must-stop place on this stretch of coast. Within easy reach of the Channel Islands, and with two first-class marinas and packed with atmosphere and history, it is somewhere you won't want to miss.

NAVIGATION

From whichever direction you choose to approach St Malo, you should by now be familiar with the joys, or otherwise, of navigation in this part of France, with fast-flowing tides, large tidal ranges and an abundance of rocky outcrops. The main approach from NW, the Chenal de la Petite Porte, is straightforward it you pay great attention to the buoyage. From other directions, it calls for a bit more nerve.

There are two marinas. Port Vauban will have you moored at the foot of the city walls, and you must lock in – roughly 2 hr either side of HW or at advertised times. There are traffic lights, which you must respect.

The Port des Bas Sablons has no lock, but a sill, which you won't be able to cross a couple of hours either side of LW. There is a depth gauge.

OVERVIEW

The original walls were built at the end of the 17th century under the direction of the great military architect, Vauban. The place was more or less flattened in the Second World War and what you see is a complete reconstruction. If you didn't know it you wouldn't

▼ For a quieter time, the waterfront close by Les Bas Sablons offers a refuge from the bustle of St Malo

The essentials:

Port Vauban

AMENITIES 50 visitor berths, but most visitors are found a space somewhere, even if you have to raft in high season.

FUEL Diesel on the marina (also waste oil disposal).

REPAIRS Capitainerie will advise. Many companies close-by offering lift-out, storage, servicing, all repairs.

FACILITIES (No token needed) and toilets alongside the Bureau du Port. These facilities are not the most modern.

LAUNDRY On the marina, or Laverie Rocabey, 27 blvd. de la Tour d'Auvergne (20 min walk).

HIRE Cycle hire at Les Vélos Bleus, 19 rue Alphonse Thébault (15 min walk).

Port des Bas Sablons

AMENITIES On the marina – on the walkway from the eastern-most pontoons, the furthest from the visitor pontoons. Try to get a berth as close to the shore as possible to avoid ferry wash and incoming swell in W/NW winds. A short walk to the ferry terminal.

REPAIRS Port Vauban is better for repairs and engineers. Volvo engine dealership.

CHANDLERY Close by.

FACILITIES Both ashore and on pontoon B (no showers, no laundry).

LAUNDRY In St Servan, 17 rue des Bas Sablons (10 min walk, behind the beach).

CLUB There is a yacht club above the capitainerie (glass-fronted building).

▼ Traditional ships are regular visitors. No shortage of maritime history here

guess – they've managed to rebuild the atmosphere into the reconstructed granite walls and the narrow cobbled streets.

In the 6th century, a monastic settlement was founded here by followers of Brendan the Navigator. St Malo himself, who was a disciple of Brendan, came from Wales, his reputation having been gained after performing miracles as a boy. There are many churches in Brittany named after him. The *Tro Breizh* ('Tour of Brittany' in Breton) is a pilgrimage that celebrates their founding saints, of which Malo was one.

In the 19th century, this was a place of privateers and pirates. Now, the bustling tourist industry has devised more benign ways of taking your money.

Although now part of the same commune, St Servan, to the south, can be considered a town in its own right, known for its parks and gardens, as well as shops (better for provisions than St Malo) and, some say, better seafood restaurants – convenient if you choose to moor in Port des Bas Sablons, which is close to the beach at the head of the bay.

Have no fear of being weather-bound in and around St Malo – there is much to distract you.

THINGS TO SEE AND DO
St Malo (distances from Port Vauban)
Museé de la Ville, Place Châteaubriand (5 min walk) tells the story of St Malo with ship models and paintings in a castle once owned by the dukes of Brittany.

Walk the walls – you can do a complete circuit of the city walls with

▼ Vauban, the great military architect, inspired much of St Malo's original architecture

plenty of opportunities to dive off and enjoy the nearby beach and fantastic views.

The **Grand Aquarium**, rue du Gén Patton (15 min by taxi or bus No 1 from the train station – see below) houses 11,000 marine animals and 600 species. Signage in English, touch pools for children, simulated submarine dive.

Cathédrale St Vincent, Place Jean de Châtillon (10 min walk) was originally built during the 12th and 18th centuries but severely damaged in the Second World War. It was reconsecrated in 1972. A plaque marks the spot in 1535 where the explorer Jacques Cartier was blessed by the bishop before setting off on the voyage that would eventually lead to the discovery of Canada.

You can walk out to **Île du Grand Bé** at LW (check the tide!), the burial place of the 18th-century writer François-René de Chateaubriand.

▼ The peaceful Anse de Solidor, south of the Bas Sablons marina – a short walk

St Servan (distances from Port des Bas Sablons)

The **Cape Horn Museum**, Quai Sébastopol (10 min walk) is housed in the Solidor Tower, built in the 14th century as a fortification for the dukes of Brittany. It gave control to the entrance of the River Rance. At one time it served as the local jail. There are good views from the top, and a lively celebration of the Cape Horn pioneers and Breton explorers, many of whom would have set sail from St Malo.

Mémorial 39–45 Fort de la Cité d'Alet, Espl. 83e DI Américaine Août 44 (10 min walk) is an 18th-century fort taken over by the Germans in the war, and now tells the story of the battles here. There are some tours in English.

Mont St Michel

This has been a place of pilgrimage for centuries, the abbey having its origins as far back as AD 966, and is a UNESCO World Heritage Site. It has been and continues to be a seat of learning and cultural inspiration.

It is a great tragedy that the grand bay in which this inspiring island stands makes it near impossible for yachts to visit with ease. The island is only 2.8 hectares (7 acres) and just 1km (0.6 miles) from the shore, but this is a place of shifting sands and big tides and an approach is not to be recommended.

However, it is not to be missed and an excursion from St Malo is the best bet.

There is more than a thousand years of history here, and over 2 million visitors a year. This is not a relic but a working abbey, with nearly 50 monks and nuns resident in the village. The place was built for devotion and contemplation, and not tourism, so expect steep steps and narrow pathways.

There is a small entrance fee to the abbey, but not to access the island. You'll find a maritime museum and a parish church with a cemetery.

▼ St Malo is great for wandering, shopping and feeding yourself

There is a bus service from St Malo (37km/23 miles). Look for Flixbus, although there are plenty of alternatives offering coach services. The cheapest tickets are available from 4 euros (Central Bus Station, near the SNCF station, Esplanade de la Bourse).

FOOD AND SHOPPING

St Malo

● **Carrefour City**, 10 rue Ste-Barbe (5 min walk). St Malo is not the best place for food shopping, except for **seafood**, and you'll have to hunt for the basement supermarket. Stays open late.

● Look out for a **bakery** just inside the main gate coming from the Vauban marina. Reports speak of no croissants being available till 0800, but worth the wait.

● Further on through the main gate, straight ahead, a couple of shops on the right lies a better bakery for **bread**.

St Servan

● **Les Halles**, 80 rue Georges Clemenceau (15 min walk).
● **Carrefour City**, 17 rue Ville Pépin (15 min walk).
● **Market day** – Tuesday and Friday in St Malo at Place de la Poissonnerie, the name of the location giving a strong clue to the fine seafood on offer here. The crab comes highly recommended. Also Tuesday and Friday at Place Bouvet, St Servan.

FURTHER AFIELD

St Malo is an excellent place to organise a crew change. Brittany Ferries offers daily sailings to Portsmouth. There is a shuttle ferry between St Malo and Dinard (10 min). Ferry service with Condor Ferries to Jersey (1 hr 20 min) and to Guernsey (3 hr).

Train station: ave. Anita Conti (40 min walk from Port des Bas Sablons, 20 min from Port Vauban). Trains pass through Rennes with connections to all parts of northern France and a direct high-speed connection to Paris (2 hr 15 min), making it possible to connect to Eurostar and London.

Dinard airport, 35730 Pleurtuit, is 15km (9.3 miles) from the city.

This stretch of coast is served by the MAT bus network, which operates next to the train station. Also stops in St Servan.

Tourist information
Esplanade St-Vincent (5 min walk from Port Vauban)

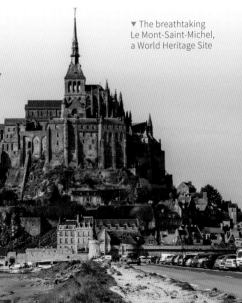

▼ The breathtaking Le Mont-Saint-Michel, a World Heritage Site

THE COTENTIN PENINSULA

GRANVILLE
▶ ST VAAST

THIS IS THE FINGER OF LAND that points north towards England, and at the same time beckons us towards France.

It's probably the most popular landfall for UK boats, given that the crossing from the Needles is around 97km (60 miles) – the second shortest crossing after Dover to Calais – and when you get there, you find the convenience of a large and safe harbour in Cherbourg, and plenty of atmospheric harbours to visit on both the peninsula's east and west sides. The western side faces the Channel Islands, making for a short hop, and this is known as the Côte des Îles, the Island Coast.

If Cherbourg is your first calling place, you might think this whole area is a place of naval shipyards, fast-moving ferries and metropolitan bustle, but there are parts of the peninsula that feel as remote as anywhere you'll find in northern France, with landscapes ranging from cliffs to moors, farmland, fields and marshes, many of which can be enjoyed from coastal footpaths. There is also the finest collection of Norman churches scattered along the length of the peninsula.

If you are French-speaking, but baffled by the language you are hearing, this is one of the few places that, because of its isolation, has allowed the Norman language to survive. There's a patriotic song you may hear, 'Sus la mé', or 'On the Sea', which is sung in traditional Norman.

The peninsula is largely driven by agriculture and not the sea, and is famed for its vegetable growing, particularly on the west-facing side. Here, you'll find the renowned and characteristic carrots from Créances – the soil there is sandy and rich in iodine, giving a sweet and deep orange carrot. Portbail is the nearest harbour.

Normandy cider and calvados are well known, made from local apples and pears, but if you are starting at St Malo and heading for Cotentin, be sure to try the salt marsh lamb, which is reared in that elbow region where the coast swings northwards, and has been since the 11th century. The marshland grazing gives a great depth of flavour to the meat due to the rich variety of herbs and grasses, which revel in the twice-daily soaking in salt water.

On the eastern side, at St Vaast la Hougue, you can indulge in the oysters – this is a very popular harbour with UK sailors – and if you wonder what hougue means, it's a Norse word for 'hill'. Yes, as with so many places along the Channel coast, the Vikings were once here.

▼ The Cotentin Peninsula is the first landfall in France for many boats coming from the UK

GRANVILLE

▲ A substantial marina, but there's pressure on space in high season

ST HELIER 30NM, ST MALO 20NM, CAP DE LA HAGUE 45NM, WEYMOUTH 110NM

Granville is sometimes called 'The Monaco of the North' due to being built on a rocky outcrop – nothing to do with wealth! It's a major yachting centre with museums, a golf course, horse racing and an aquarium.

Step off your boat and straight into a characterful town. However, there's a bleakness about the marina, with its high concrete walls. Berths might be scarce in July and August, and you have no chance when the Tour de France cycle race passes through town. However, there is lots to do whatever the weather, and for all ages.

NAVIGATION

This is the land of big tidal ranges – 12m (39ft) approx. at springs. Entrance to the marina is over a sill and illuminated signs display the depth of water. The marina has 150 visitor berths and yachts are often met by the harbour launch – the staff are generally found to be helpful.

OVERVIEW

Founded by the Vikings, Granville became a wealthy town and one of the most important in Normandy. As early as the 13th century, fishing fleets set sail from here for the fish-rich waters off Newfoundland.

The first fortifications were built in the 14th century by the English, who at that time occupied Normandy. Because of the appearance of the town's walls, Granville is often described as a small-scale St Malo. Rest assured that within the fortress walls there has

▲ A pleasant town to wander, shop and eat in

been no modernisation, by comparison
with the surrounding town, whose
character has been overwhelmed by
development. Its prosperity declined as
St Malo grew in stature but it was saved
by the coming of the Paris–Granville
railway line, which established tourism
as a new industry at a time when the
fishing fleets were declining. You
will see some grand old houses, once

belonging to Parisians who languished
here in the heat of the summer.

THINGS TO SEE AND DO

Plage du Plat Gousset is magnificent –
a long, sandy beach with a sea-water
swimming pool at LW. It lies to the
north of the marina, so head for the
town and keep going. It's a gently
shelving beach with lifeguards, so
ideal for small children.

The Christian Dior Museum, 1 rue
d'Estouteville (30 min walk) celebrates
the work of the world-famous fashion
designer, who was born here in this
villa, Les Rhumbs, in 1905. His mother

▼ Don't expect much traffic at LW!

▲ This is an important terminus for high-speed Channel Island ferries

north from the marina) has a collection of books, sculptures and paintings by the Paris bookseller Richard Anacréon.

Centre Aquatique l'Hippocampe, rue des Lycées (25 min walk) is a terrific modern swimming pool with a baby pool, diving and saunas.

If you're not feeling confident enough to take your own boat to **Îles Chausey** (365 islands at low tide and 52 at high tide) there are plenty of day trips ('Joile France') from Granville, but early booking is essential on summer weekends as it gets busy.

FOOD AND SHOPPING

● **Carrefour City**, 5 rue Clément Desmaisons (10 min walk).
● There are three restaurants on the marina. The yacht club is open to visitors but you may not find much there.
● **Market day** is Saturday in the summer. A large market with a covered area. Head for the beach and find it behind the casino. There is **fish**, **oysters** and **mussels**, and produce from local farms at Place Maréchal Foch (10 min walk).

FURTHER AFIELD

There's a train station at Place Pierre-Semard (20 min). The station is at the end of a spur that connects at Coutances. Trains to Cherbourg for a crew change (2 hr), change at Lison. Ferry service (Manche Îles Express) to St Helier (1 hr 30 min). Bus station by the railway station – buses to Paris and Normandy cities. There is a bus service Granville to Cherbourg (5 hr), changing at Valognes for a budget crew change.

was a dedicated gardener and that floral influence shows in many of Dior's designs, which are on display. Take a look at the Dior Star, his lucky star – he never took decisions without first consulting a fortune-teller. The gardens have free admission.

Seventeenth-century **Notre Dame**, rue Notre Dame (10 min walk) overlooks the sea and once served as a navigation mark. The legend, of 1113, says that fishermen found in their nets a statue of the Virgin and they took this as a sign from heaven, which initially inspired the building of this church.

Le Roc des Curiosités is a museum and aquarium, 1 blvd. Vaufleury (20 min walk, on the peninsula), housing butterflies, fish, a shell collection and a sea lion. It's famous for keeping children well amused, although it's quite small and has none of the sparkle of a modern aquarium. The shell collection and shell sculptures might be described as 'unusual'.

The **Museum of Modern Art**, La Haute-Ville, Place de l'Isthme (10 min walk

Tourist information
2 rue Lecampion (12 min walk)

CARTERET

ALDERNEY 30NM, JERSEY 25NM, GUERNSEY 30NM

This is a lovely village with dunes and a sandy beach close by, making it a popular resort. You may find its name combined with its neighbour, Barneville. There's some good coastal walking here.

NAVIGATION

Beware cross tides in the entrance. Point Carteret lighthouse helps identification and stands to the west of the breakwater. Use the latest pilotage information, as there have been reports of recent changes in the approach due to shifting sands. The marina has 60 visitor berths – you may have to raft. Look out for the traffic lights as you approach the sill. A major expansion is currently taking place.

OVERVIEW

You'll find this a quiet place if you're lucky enough to be cruising off-season, otherwise expect a throng of tourists. The harbour is known as the 'Port of the Isles' and is the nearest to Jersey. With so many places destroyed in the Second World War, Carteret was lucky in that US forces were responsible for harbour expansion, which gave us the haven we enjoy today. Barneville, part of the same commune, was built on a hill and was a fortress in medieval times and used as a coastal lookout.

▼ Set among dunes, this marina has a spacious feel to it

THINGS TO SEE AND DO

Above the beach at Carteret, a footpath – with views of the Channel Islands – follows the coast to the north, leading to the **dunes of Hatainville**. This is a remarkable piece of geography – ancient cliffs were covered in a blanket of sand 70,000 years ago, which has created unique habitat for some of the rarest coastal vegetation.

If the weather keeps you confined to Carteret, an excursion to the nearby drying harbour of **Portbail** has a lot to offer. There's a convenient tourist train that makes the 10km (6.2 mile) trip using carriages from the 1930s. Portbail is a quiet place, but full of atmosphere. The church, **Notre Dame**, is medieval, as is much of architecture around it. It's an active place and a visit to the tourist information could be rewarding – they have an annual Mardi Gras and a comedy festival. There's good walking, cycling and sand yachting here, too. The beach is named after Charles Lindbergh, who crossed it on his pioneering transatlantic flight.

FOOD AND SHOPPING

- **Boulangerie Clerot**, 6 rue de Paris (5 min walk west from the harbour office).
- Follow rue de Paris to the west to a smart **shopping street** for groceries, bakery, coffee and cafés.
- No proper supermarket in Carteret. Nearest is in **Barneville Carrefour**,

◀ **1** Good dining close by the marina; **2 & 4** The Thursday market is busy and well stocked; **3 & 6** It's a short walk from the marina to two sandy beaches with cliff-top walks and views across to the Channel Islands; **5** The helpful harbour office also serves as the tourist info

The essentials:

FUEL Available in the marina, at the reception berth below the harbour office (to port on entering).

REPAIRS Lift-out possible.

LAUNDRY No launderette, but sinks and basins in a well-maintained marina.

CLUB Yacht club de Barneville Carteret on the marina welcomes visitors.

HIRE Pre-book electric bikes at the marina office.

17 route du Pont Rose (35 min walk).
- **Market day** in Barneville is Saturday, and it can be busy.
- There is a **thriving market** in **Carteret** every Thursday on the Place du Terminus, opposite the old train station (7 min walk).

FURTHER AFIELD

There is a ferry service to both Gorey and St Helier on Jersey, and to St Peter Port on Guernsey (Manche Iles Express). The nearest railway (30km/18.6 miles) is at Valognes, with connections to Cherbourg and Paris. During the season, a tourist railway runs between Carteret and Portbail, the next harbour to the south. The bus company Manéo operates services to Cherbourg, Valognes and Coutances (in season). There's a bus stop at the Mairie, 1 Place de la Mairie (30 min walk).

Tourist information

In Barneville, 15 rue Guillaume le Conquérant (30 min walk) or in Carteret, 3 ave. de la République (5 min walk west from the marina)

DIÉLETTE

GUERNSEY 28NM, **ALDERNEY** 15NM, **CHERBOURG** 30NM, **ST MALO** 60NM

This is the nearest French harbour to Guernsey and therefore popular with both sailors and those who use the ferry service between the two. You may find less charm here than in some other towns – it has a considerable industrial history of mining and quarrying and these days nuclear power, unmissable to the south of the harbour.

NAVIGATION

Tides are approaching a 12m (39ft) range at springs. There are two marinas: the first, on the left, is the Bassin de Commerce (from where ferries leave) with visitor moorings, and a further basin to the south is separated by a sill. Read the tide gauges with care. Be cautious entering in strong onshore winds.

OVERVIEW

Although a decent harbour and a well-kept marina, there is not much else here apart from a wine shop, a couple of bars, a café and a kebab house. For anything more than that it's a walk to nearby Flamanville, which is 30 minutes away up a steep hill, but pleasant walking. Thankfully, a headland blocks the view of the power station from the marina.

THINGS TO SEE AND DO

If the children are finding few attractions here, try **Ferme aux 5 Saisons**, rue des Moliers, Flamanville (10 min by taxi or 45 min walk) an interactive farm with animals, bread baking and golf! There is an occasional **fun fair** to the south of the marina.

▼ The marina restaurant might be the best bet, unless you are up for a lengthy walk to the nearby town of Flamanville

▼ This is a good and safe marina, but not much going on around it

FOOD AND SHOPPING

- For bread, croissants etc try **Boulangerie Richy** in Flamanville to the south, rue des Longs Champs (40 min walk).
- **Cocci Supermarket** (modest) on the road to Flamanville, 66 route de Diélette (25 min walk). **Pharmacie** next door.
- Vivéco (mini-mart), 9 rue du Château in Flamanville (40 min walk).
- Useful **wine shop** on the marina.

FURTHER AFIELD

There are ferries from here to Alderney (55 min) and Guernsey (1 hr 10 min) but limited sailings. Operated by Manche Iles Express.

Tourist information
None

The essentials:

AMENITIES The harbour office is on the eastern side of the Bassin de Commerce – it's bright red.

FUEL The fuel berth is on the western side of the sill between the two basins.

REPAIRS 40T Travelift. For repair advice, try the clubhouse at Centre Nautique de Diélette, western side of the inner harbour.

LAUNDRY On the marina.

▲ Good facilities here for lifting, and good hard standing

▽ Entrance to Cherbourg, a military base with huge fortifications

▷ Umbrellas still flying in Cherbourg, 60 years after the award-winning film *Umbrellas of Cherbourg*

CHERBOURG

LE HAVRE 70NM, NEEDLES 60NM, BRIGHTON 90NM, GUERNSEY 40NM

Probably the most visited of the French channel ports by south coast sailors, Cherbourg can be thought of as the 'capital' of the Cotentin peninsula. It's a safe harbour, easily entered, with a well-run marina with all facilities and a bustling town. It's a great place to start a cruise of the French Channel coast.

NAVIGATION

The harbour is hard to miss with its impressive fortifications. The marina lies behind a second sea wall, which creates the Petite Rade on the southern side of the harbour. There are no dangers in the approach, with the possible exception of the tide, which runs at speed along this headland.

There are no fewer than 300 visitor berths here and, given the majority of the visiting clientele, you'll find English spoken well in the capitainerie.

OVERVIEW

Napoleon was responsible for the transformation of Cherbourg from a rather indifferent harbour into the fortress we see today. He did this by building lengthy stone breakwaters, complete with forts, to provide a safe and secure haven for his fleets and to make an invasion impossible. There remains a considerable French naval base here, although it is much reduced in recent years. There is a statue of Napoleon, atop a horse, with a reminder of his declared intention that in this place he would 'recreate

the wonders of Egypt'. You can judge for yourself the success of that.

The area around Cherbourg is the first place in France in which the Vikings made a successful invasion in the 9th century. In the 20th century, transatlantic sea travel was a major business; the *Titanic,* on her maiden and ill-fated voyage, stopped here to take on passengers after leaving Southampton. She was lost five days later.

In both world wars, Cherbourg was of huge strategic importance as a supply port to the British forces fighting in France in the First World War, and then a main focus of the Allied D-Day invasion on 6 June 1944. The port had been completely destroyed but amazing efforts by French and American engineers brought it back into operation; by the end of the war it had traffic double that of New York City.

THINGS TO SEE AND DO

La Cité de la Mer Museum, Allée du Président Menut, is clearly visible from the marina to the east, but there's

▼ Visitors from the UK always welcome in Cherbourg's spacious marina

The essentials:

FUEL Berth opposite the capitainerie.

REPAIRS All repairs including engines, sails, gear, GRP work can be achieved here.

FACILITIES Showers and toilets at the capitainerie.

LAUNDRY On the marina, or Laverie Libre Service, 35 rue du Val de Saire (15 min walk across the bridge, past the tourist information).

HIRE Cycle hire at VRC Giant Cherbourg, Parc de la Belle Jardinière 2 (15 min taxi ride to the east towards Querqueville).

SWIMMING POOL Piscine Chantereyne – public pool at rue du Diablotin (5 min walk, part of the marina complex).

a 25 min walk to get there. Without doubt the first stopping place if sailing with children is this **science and history museum** in the impressive art deco former transatlantic liner terminal. You can discover the *Titanic* story and board France's first nuclear submarine, and there is a ride in a submarine simulator. Press noses up close to the 17 tanks in the aquarium, which hold 4,000 marine creatures.

Cherbourg is not blessed with beaches and to find one you'll have to head west to **Querqueville** to find a long, sandy beach with children's playgrounds (20 min by taxi). The **Plage de Sciotot** is reckoned to be the best beach, but is even further west and a 20 min taxi ride from the marina.

The **Parc Emmanuel Liais,** rue Emmanuel Liais, has free entry and consists of hundreds of plant species collected by a former mayor of Cherbourg (15 min walk).

Need an umbrella? Cherbourg umbrellas are famous largely due to the 1964 movie *The Umbrellas of Cherbourg*. The factory is open for tours, 22 Quai Alexandre-III (20 min walk).

The Fort of Roul was built at the time for Napoleon to protect the harbour but now contains the **Liberation Museum**, Mnt des Résistants (40 min walk, 15 min by taxi). It tells the story of the German occupation and the eventual liberation. There's a good view of the harbour.

▲ Emperor Napoleon the 1st of France – responsible for the creation of this formidable harbour

FOOD AND SHOPPING

- You will find limitless food shopping as you wander from the marina into the town, with **bakeries**, **butchers** and **fruit shops**. The main shopping streets are rue Tour-Carrée and rue de la Paix.
- For large-scale shopping, the nearest **hypermarket**, Carrefour Cherbourg, is opposite the rail station at the southern end of the inner harbour (20 min walk).
- **CocciMarket** is a small but useful supermarket, 17 Place de la Révolution (10 min walk).
- To the west of the quayside, in the old town, is a network of pavements and alleys lined with **shops**.
- There are **numerous markets** held throughout the week in Cherbourg. The Thursday market is generally considered the most important in the place du Général-de-Gaulle (15 min walk). There is a Sunday market on ave. de Normandie (10 min by taxi). If you hunt around, you'll find some kind of market on every day of the week. The **flower market** is on Saturday mornings.

FURTHER AFIELD

There are regular ferry connections to Portsmouth and Poole (Brittany Ferries) in the UK, and to Rosslare and Dublin in Ireland. The ferry port, 50100 Cherbourg, is found to the east of the marina (10 min by taxi, 40 min on foot).

The rail station, Gare de Cherbourg, is at the southern end of the inner harbour, ave. Jean François Millet (10 min by taxi or a 30 min walk). Trains go to Paris (approx. 1 hr 30 min) or to Rennes (approx. 4 hr). Trains to Bayeux to view the tapestry (55 min) and Lille (5 hr) to change for Eurostar.

The nearest airport is Mauperus, 11km (7 miles) east of Cherbourg, 7 rue Jean Mermoz (30 min by taxi). This is a former military airfield with no scheduled flights. The main bus station is close by the rail station (above) with routes to Paris, Rennes, Caen, Paris airports.

Tourist information
14 Quai Alexandre-III (13 min walk)

ST VAAST
LA HOUGUE

CARENTAN 18NM, **COURSEULLES-SUR-MER** 35NM, **CHERBOURG** 22NM,
PORTSMOUTH 70NM, **POOLE** 72NM

This is a hugely popular harbour with UK south coast sailors, with a secure and safe marina and good walks to Île de Tatihou at LW. It's also a pleasant town to stroll.

NAVIGATION

The marina is approached through a lock gate but if you are early on the tide, and the wind is W, there is anchorage outside. There are rocky outcrops south of Île de Tatihou and the buoyage should be followed with care. If anchoring, be aware of oyster beds and crab/lobster pots in the approach.

OVERVIEW

This is an important oyster-growing region, and an extremely popular tourist centre in the lee of the Cherbourg peninsula, known for its gentler weather. There are LW walks to islands, a botanical garden and a maritime museum. The fortified towers on Île de Tatihou and Fort de la Hougue

▼ Traditional boatbuilding and restoration here

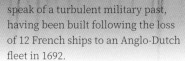

▼ It's a lengthy walk to the town until the lock gates closes and it becomes a short trip

speak of a turbulent military past, having been built following the loss of 12 French ships to an Anglo-Dutch fleet in 1692.

It was not until 1982 that the lock gates were built, which transformed a drying harbour into a popular cruising destination. There is much activity ashore, but wandering the town with its multiplicity of shops, cafés and restaurants can easily use up a whole day.

The essentials: ⚓

FUEL All the facilities you could wish for here, including diesel, engineers, haul-out and hard standing.

CHANDLERY USHIP, 5 rue de Réville on the marina, north end. St Vaast Marine (mostly small boats and outboards), 1 Chemin des Coûts (10 min walk). Chantier Naval Bernard, top-class boatyard working wood, steel, GRP, 4 Place du Général Leclerc (10 min walk).

FACILITIES The capitainerie is close to the lock gate on the right as you enter. There are well-appointed showers, toilets and a launderette.

THINGS TO SEE AND DO

St Vaast le Hougue

At Île Tatihou, visitor numbers are limited to 500 a day. You can travel here on foot at LW by carefully making your way across the oyster beds, or at other states of tide take the remarkable amphibious water bus – the booking office is near the marina, where you must buy tickets in advance. This bus/boat is great fun for children. The Vauban tower on the island is UNESCO listed. The island's maritime museum was created in 1992 with collections of artefacts from the many battles that took place here as far back as 1692, the date of the Battle of La Hougue in

▼ An active fishing fleet. Expect to have to tread between drying nets

▼ Good beach, many rock pools to the south of the town – Vauban la Hougue in the distance

which the French were defeated, hence the building of the two impressive forts. There are three gardens on the island, the largest being a maritime garden. There is also a bird reserve as this is an important stopping place for migrant birds. The **Tatihou Maritime Museum**, La Tour Tatihou, has creative activities for children, and there is a world music festival in August.

Vauban de la Hougue

This is considered a splendid example of Vauban architecture and is found on a spit of land to the south of the town. When both this tower, and the one on Tatihou, were completed, Vauban, the 15th-century French military engineer, described this as being 'the safest in the entire kingdom'. It is free to access during the summer season. There is a good beach here, tennis courts, a children's playground and a beach café, La Hougette.

La Chapelle des Marins, 5585A Place du Général Leclerc (10 min walk) is close to the boatyard. This chapel dates from the 11th century but what you see today owes much to the 16th century. It is dedicated to those who have lost their lives at sea.

It is unusual for a shop to be listed among distinguished tourist attractions, but **Maison Gosselin**, 27 rue de Verrue (5 min walk) is no ordinary shop, although you may not recognise it as such at first sight. You enter what you believe to be a rather ordinary mini-mart, but you soon go into a sequence of smaller rooms, one selling

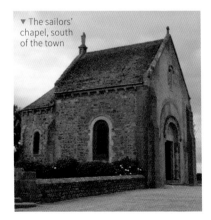
▼ The sailors' chapel, south of the town

freshly ground coffee, then calvados, then fine wines, delicatessen, cigars ... it goes on and on. Eventually you arrive in the functional back yard where orders are piled up waiting for delivery, yours among them. Just to add to the exotic mix, you might find children's toys and buckets and spades. Do not miss this shop.

Although **Barfleur** on the NE tip of the Cotentin peninsula is a drying harbour, a day out from St Vaast will be rewarded with a real Normandy experience. The town is almost an open-air museum in its own right. It is difficult to believe that this was once a major port centuries ago, with a population of almost 10,000 people. In 1120, King Henry I of England and 300 others set sail from here towards England after a visit. It is recorded that 'the carelessness of the intoxicated crew drove her onto a rock'. All hands were lost, including Henry's male heir, which resulted in eventual civil war in England.

Barfleur is on the official list of 'most beautiful villages in France'. The 17th-century church, Sainte Catherine, vies for prominence with the 71m (233ft)-tall lighthouse on the headland.

FOOD AND SHOPPING

- For **bread**, Boulangerie Gibon, 2 rue Froide (2 min walk).
- Also, **patisserie** on the road alongside the marina with many eating and drinking opportunities. Good **seafood outlets**.
- Numerous **grocery shops** in town,
- but for major shopping try **the market**, 1 rue Marcel Pignot (15 min walk, 5 min by taxi).
- There's a **street market** Saturday morning till midday.

FURTHER AFIELD

The nearest train station is Valognes (20 min by taxi) – trains to Cherbourg and in the direction of Paris (3 hr). Ferries to Portsmouth from Cherbourg.

Tourist information
1 Place du Général de Gaulle
(5 min walk towards the landward
end of the marina)

▼ Is it a truck ... or a boat? The amphibious ferry to Tatihou

D-DAY BEACHES OF NORMANDY

CARENTAN ▶ HONFLEUR

YOU CANNOT FULLY APPRECIATE this length of low-lying coastline and its wide sandy beaches without first having an understanding of the importance of D-Day (6 June 1944).

This was the largest and most complex military operation of all time. The relics of that day are scattered along these Normandy beaches, the war memorials are plentiful, and there are many museums that tell the tale of that great turning point in the Second World War.

The literature of these times is littered with the code names of the landing beaches, Omaha, Juno, Gold, Sword and Utah among them, and the Pegasus Bridge, which assumed huge strategic importance. But what made the Normandy beaches so convenient for Allied forces makes

it difficult for sailors. Many of the harbour approaches here dry out to a considerable distance offshore and you'll have to sail as far as Honfleur before you find a harbour entrance with plenty of water at all states of tide. But, of course, long and wide sandy beaches were exactly what the military planners were looking for, and here they found the perfect spots.

Further to the east, stretching from Ouistreham in the west to Honfleur on the Seine estuary is the Côte Fleurie, or 'Flowery Coast'. Its name is derived from the richness of the gardens attached to the villas that sprang up here during the belle époque, in the late 19th century, when parts of this coast were discovered by rich Parisians. You will see, and enjoy, many of the villas they built – some monstrous but all intriguing. These are particularly evident at Deauville and Trouville, which are probably the smartest places.

Heading eastwards, you come to Honfleur, which should be on everyone's itinerary. It sits at the mouth of the River Seine and was a major defensive port in the 15th century, protecting Paris. There is art and culture here, and much medieval atmosphere, which provides a sharp contrast with the 20th-century military echoes of those famous beaches to the west.

There's not much drama in the landscape of the hinterland, but that's what makes it so good for farming. They produce good milk here so be sure to taste as many Normandy cheeses as you can, made with milk from richly green meadows. Orchards here are packed with cherries, pears and apples, which feed the cider and Calvados industries.

Normandy has something of a reputation for the size of its meals. The Normans like their food. To aid their digestion, they introduced the 'Norman Gap', a pause between substantial courses to allow the stomach to settle and a nip of Calvados to be taken.

▼ Peaceful now, but the beaches of Normandy still bear the scars of the D-Day invasion of 1944

CARENTAN

CHERBOURG 40NM, **ST VAAST** 20NM, **LE HAVRE** 50NM,
NAB TOWER 75NM

Of the three harbours in the Baie du Grand Vey, this is the one to go for, with perfect shelter in a locked marina and the most appealing of the towns hereabouts. Walt Disney's family hailed from here.

NAVIGATION

Timing here is key – you need to get the tides right to cross the shallow and winding approach in safety, and again in the river to catch the gate opening times. The long, thin marina is beyond locked gates. A tidal bore has been reported in the river at certain states of tide.

OVERVIEW

Carentan marks the eastern beginnings of the Cotentin peninsula and is set in a watery landscape of marshes and water meadows with lush grazing for the famous dairy herds of this region. The town lies on the River Douve, part of which you will have travelled along to get here. This is one of the towns that forms a backdrop to the D-Day Normandy beaches, and it suffered huge damage as a consequence. Carentan was the meeting point of four roads and a railroad, so of huge strategic significance, and the German army fought hard to hold it. There is

▼ A modest, quiet but stately little town

▲ …but once inside a peaceful and secure spot to moor, short walk to the town

high ground to the SE and SW, which gave the German army another strategic advantage they did not wish to lose. All-night artillery bombardment from naval ships gave cover for the final assault by Allied forces.

THINGS TO SEE AND DO

To understand the kind of fighting to which this area was subject, the **Normandy Victory Museum** (near the village of Catz, 10 min by taxi), which is halfway between Isigny-sur-Mer and Carentan, is to be found on an old airfield, complete with tank rides and depictions of the close-quarters fighting here, known as the Battle of the Hedgerows.

The **D-Day Experience** near the village of St-Côme-du-Mont (10 min by taxi north out of Carentan) is a 3D movie experience and aircraft simulator.

Dead Man's Corner Museum, 2 Village de l'Amont, is housed in what was once the headquarters of the German paratroopers (the building was given that sombre name because the locals believed it to be haunted). A 40km (25 mile)-long trail gives you the chance to retrace the footsteps of the invading forces. This is probably the most immersive of all the D-Day museums in Normandy. Very good outing for families.

> ## The essentials:
>
> FUEL At the far end of the marina.
>
> REPAIRS Travelift and hard standing. The boatyard will advise on repairs.
>
> FACILITIES The capitainerie is at the far end of the marina (single-storey building) with showers and laundry.

▼ Approach through a flat landscape of rich green water meadows

FOOD AND SHOPPING

- **Carrefour Express**, 6–8 rue du Dr Caillard (10 min walk).
- **Intermarché SUPER hypermarket**, rue de la Guinguette (25 min walk).
- **Bakeries, groceries, fruit and veg** at many small shops in the town. The walk from the marina is not uplifting but the town centre has a good atmosphere when you get there.
- **Market day** is Monday, all day.

FURTHER AFIELD

The main Cherbourg–Paris rail line stops at Carentan, so there are connections to all parts of France. SNCF station: 50500 Carentan les Marais (15 min walk).

If leaving a boat here (very secure), a ferry back to the UK from Cherbourg is convenient (1 hr by taxi, 35 min by train).

> Tourist information
> 24 Place de la République
> (10 min walk)

▼ An austere welcome to the lock-protected marina…

GRANDCAMP-MAISY

PORT-EN-BESSIN 12NM, **ST VAAST** 14NM, **CHERBOURG** 35NM, **HONFLEUR** 45NM

There are three harbours in the Baie du Grand Vey, and this is the most easterly. You will find none of the tourist glamour of harbours further east or west. Some find this work-a-day atmosphere appealing. There's a good beach here with supervised swimming.

NAVIGATION

A drying entrance over a flat, rocky seabed to a locked basin. No waiting moorings or pontoon on the seaward side of the lock, so time your arrival to fit the lock opening times.

The essentials:

AMENITIES Harbour office in the SW corner of the harbour.

FUEL None on the harbour but take the D514 towards Isigny to find a filling station (24 hr) at Carrefour Contact on the first roundabout out of town (7 min walk).

CHANDLERY Also on the E side of the harbour, close to the bank. Gam Marine (chandlery) on W side of harbour. Omaha Marine at S end of harbour, but mostly geared for fishing boat work.

▼ Spacious and secure in a locked basin in the middle of the town

2

3

4

5

OVERVIEW

Like so many towns and villages along this coast, Grandcamp-Maisy's history is dominated by the events of the Second World War (see below). It was designated part of Omaha beach. There is an active fishing fleet, but yachts are welcome.

THINGS TO SEE AND DO

Maisy Battery, 7 Les Perruques (25 min walk, on the D514 towards Isigny – signposts to it are small) was the scene of a five-hour battle to disable this German stronghold. The US Army rangers formed the assault force, but until 2006 there was no recognition of their heroism

You can walk through 4km (2.5 miles) of German trenches and enter the bunkers and shelters. This is described as one of the best-kept secrets in Normandy because, until you are close to it, it remains largely invisible. The German forces kept firing for three solid days before the advancing US forces overran them. The beach uncovers quite a distance at LW and is cleaned every day in summer. It lies to the east of the harbour mouth.

▲ Spacious and secure in a locked basin in the middle of the town

FOOD AND SHOPPING

● **Carrefour Contact** (see fuel for location) (7 min walk).
● **Market day** is Tuesday, Saturday and Sunday in the town centre, with **fresh fish** on the quay most days.

FURTHER AFIELD

The nearest rail station is at Bayeux (1 hr 10 min by bus, three times a day). The nearest airport to this part of the French coast is at Caen (1 hr by taxi). Flights only within France.

A bus service running twice daily (route 70) will take you eastwards to visit Omaha beach (40 min) or take a taxi (approx. 30 euros).

◀ **1&4** A very floral and decorated little town; **2** The World Peace Statue stands at the entrance to the town; **3** Many businesses take their names from the famous Second World War landing beaches; **5** The approach is over a long, flat seabed, which dries at LW

Tourist information
26 Quai Crampon (10 min walk to the beach on the eastern side of the harbour)

PORT-EN-BESSIN

COURSEULLES-SUR-MER 12NM, **LE HAVRE** 35NM, **ST VAAST** 25NM, **NEEDLES** 85NM

There is no marina or special facilities for yachts, but don't let that put you off. Port-en-Bessin offers a taste of Normandy without the tourist veneer.

NAVIGATION

This is a drying harbour with a locked basin, dangerous in strong onshore winds. No dangers in the offing but rocky outcrops in the outer harbour. A signal station to the east of the harbour is easily spotted. A short pontoon has been established to your right after the lock gate.

OVERVIEW

This is a fishing harbour with no special facilities for yachts, and tourism has made little inroad. It was an important place during the D-Day landings as it sits between Omaha beach (US) and Gold beach (UK). Petrol and oil storage depots, serviced by offshore pipelines, were established here, giving the town great strategic importance. Cliffs on either side give it added protection. Its lack of tourist development is what makes it attractive. You'll find plenty of jolly eating places around the harbour.

THINGS TO SEE AND DO

This is not a place for tourist attractions so there is little laid on for you. It is a place to walk, eat and enjoy. It might be worth making a walking detour to the old fishermen's quarter with its 19th-century houses.

◄ A strong working atmosphere along a harbour front with many bars and cafés

► A large, modern fish market near the harbour mouth

The essentials:

FUEL You'll need to carry it from a filling station. There is fuel at the Super U (12 min walk south from the basin).

REPAIRS Chandlery and boatyard at the southern end, although geared towards fishing boat repairs.

LAUNDRY A useful conjunction of LK Electronique Marine, Lavomatique (laundrette) and bakery, all next to each other on the western side at the far end of the basin. Also a fish market here on Tuesday and Sunday mornings (6 min walk).

Note: there is no water, electricity or showers in the harbour.

FOOD AND SHOPPING

● **Modest supermarket**, 6 rue de Bayeux (2 min walk towards the lock).
● **U Express**, ave. du Général de Gaulle (12 min walk).
● **Market day** is Sunday but there's an **evening market** on Fridays in July and August, sometimes with fireworks.

FURTHER AFIELD

No train station here but there is a bus service – route AO70RV to Bayeaux (20 min).

Tourist information
Quai Baron Gérard (7 min walk)

▼ The town, with its fishing fleet at its heart

COURSEULLES-SUR-MER

OUISTREHAM 10NM, LE HAVRE 25NM, ST VAAST 35NM, PORTSMOUTH 90NM

This is a small but very popular resort, beloved of the Parisians who have second homes here, hence a certain amount of style around the place, and it is not without charm. It is, however, quiet out of season. Some come here to reflect on the D-Day events on Juno beach.

NAVIGATION

The harbour has a drying entrance and off-lying dangers, some of which may be awash at LW. The lock to the Bassin Joinville opens HW +–2. Visitor

▼ Fresh fish is always for sale on the quayside

moorings (30) are on the eastern side of the basin. The harbour office is halfway along the marina on the western side – there are showers and toilets here. At LW the harbour can be pungent.

OVERVIEW

This is where the River Seulles meets the sea. It is a compact town so walking distances are modest, and there are many shopping opportunities. There is also much scope for entertaining children, and the beach is top class. Although it has been a port since Roman times, and has a reputation for its oysters, like so many small harbours along this stretch of coast it is remembered largely for its part in the D-Day landings in 1944. The beach here was codenamed Juno, and there was

---

The essentials:

FUEL None on the marina. Ask for directions to nearest garage.

CHANDLERY Quai Ouest Marine, 8 Chemin de la Tuilerie (7 min walk).

LAUNDRY Lavomatique near the Place du Marché, close to the useful Central Café (10 min).

▲ No hazards in the approach, apart from the falling tide!

considerable loss of Canadian life here. It was the first harbour in Normandy to be liberated.

THINGS TO SEE AND DO

Juno Beach Centre, Voie des Français Libres (10 min) is a complete Second World War experience focused on the events on Juno beach, which it overlooks. It was opened in 2003, inspired by veterans and volunteers who wanted to pay tribute to the 359 Canadians who lost their lives here on D-Day, and the 45,000 total who were lost in the war. Exhibitions are designed for all ages, in French and English, and many of them are interactive.

Les Jardins de la Mer is a pleasant park close by.

The Cross of Lorraine is a steel structure overlooking Juno beach. It commemorates General de Gaulle's return to French soil in 1944. The cross was the symbol of the Free French and was displayed on warships and aircraft.

The beach off the town, **Juno**, was one of five beaches designated as landing places for the Allied D-Day invasion. To fully appreciate the scale of planning that went into the D-Day operation, a visit to Arromanches, 16km (10 miles) to the west, is worthwhile. There is no harbour of any kind here so one was created out of floating concrete, known as a Mulberry harbour, to provide protection for the invading forces. It was a bold and successful piece of military engineering. The remains are still visible and yachts have anchored among them, mindful of the unmarked

▼ Yachts live side by side with the fishing fleet here

debris that lies on the seabed. The **D-Day museum** here is packed with information, all well displayed in both English and French.

FOOD AND SHOPPING

- **Boulangerie** on the E quayside.
- **Carrefour City**, 59 rue de la Mer (10 min walk).
- Many **food outlets** at all prices and to suit all tastes around the marina, and in the town.
- **Market days** are Tuesday and Friday in the **Place du Marché** (covered market planned for 2021); Sunday morning market in the **harbour** July and August (10 min walk).
- **Fish market** every day on the quay.

FURTHER AFIELD

No railway station. There is no bus route that will sweep you the length of this remarkable piece of military history, but most harbours in this region have a bus service to Bayeaux for the beaches and the tapestry.

Bus to Caen (1 hr 15 min) bus stop at 16 Place du Six Juin (4 min walk). The No 70 bus from the railway station takes you to the American Cemetery at Pointe du Hoc (30 min). The No 74 bus takes you to Arromanches (20 min). Check Bus Verts online for local buses along the length of Normandy's beaches.

Nearest ferries to UK Ouistreham (30 min by taxi), Le Havre (1 hr 45 min), Cherbourg (1 hr 40 min).

Tourist information

5 rue du 11 Novembre (7 min walk)

▶ **1** The harbour entrance, almost dry at LW; **2** Cinema; **3** Yacht Club; **4** Second World War relics on proud display by the harbour – Duplex Drive Sherman Tank; **5** A fine example of a Normandy Beach; **6** The seafront has everything needed to keep a family happy for a day

1

2 COURSEULLES·SUR·MER
CINEMA

3 YACHT CLUB

4

5

6

OUISTREHAM/ CAEN

ST VAAST 45NM, **LE HAVRE** 18NM, **NAB TOWER** 85NM

Ouistreham, the arrival place for the Portsmouth ferry (Brittany Ferries), is a quiet spot at the mouth of the River Orne, which leads to Caen (15km/9.3 miles inland), passing the site of the Second World War battle for Pegasus Bridge (see below). There's good walking, a fine sandy beach and a casino here, and much wartime history. But this is a routine kind of town, which acts as a gateway for those taking the ferry to and from Portsmouth. The marina, on the opposite bank to the town, is sheltered from all weathers, making it a convenient place to leave a boat if you have to take a ferry back to the UK.

NAVIGATION

The tide is set strongly across the entrance, but apart from that it's quite straightforward. Entry to the marina is via a lock but there is an all-tide waiting pontoon on the seaward side. Not many landmarks to indicate arrival apart from the lighthouse Oc.WR 4s.

OVERVIEW

Trading has occurred from here since the Middle Ages but it was the D-Day assault of 6 June 1944 on Sword beach that wrote this place into the history books. Allied soldiers fought their way inland to the Pegasus Bridge on the way to Caen, which was captured by soldiers dropped in by glider in one of

▼ Long sandy beaches to the east and west of the town

the first D-Day actions. This raid slowed the German counter-attack from the east, hence its importance. *The Longest Day* (1962) was filmed in Port-en-Bessin and tells the story. The original Pegasus Bridge, previously called the Bénouville Bridge after the nearby village, was removed to the museum at Ranville and is now a war memorial.

The beaches to the west, furthest from the marina, are more popular than those to the east.

CAEN

Take the canal from Ouistreham to Caen and you find yourself in a very different world. Ouistreham is definitely rural, whereas Caen is a bustling city with a town centre marina, which is perfectly secure but the roar of the city might disturb the peace somewhat. It is a short walk from the marina to the castle, which now houses a Museum of Normandy and hosts cultural events. All shopping needs can be met in central Caen.

▲ A peaceful marina at Ouistreham, useful if leaving the boat

The essentials:

FUEL In the marina.

REPAIRS/CHANDLERY Available through the marina.

LAUNDRY Launderette on the marina, or La Belle Laverie, 2 ave. Pasteur (25 min walk).

HIRE The tourist authority has a fleet of 20 bicycles spread around its offices. E-bikes are available for half days upwards from stationbees.com (they have a pick-up point in Ouistreham). Cycleways are expanding here – check with tourist information.

Note: it is feature of this place that most things are a decent walk from the marina and many of the places you might wish to visit are on the west side of the canal.

▼ The entrance to the canal, looking seaward from Ouistreham

THINGS TO SEE AND DO

Caen is 15km (9.3 miles) inland but starting at Ouistreham there are **splendid walks** along the canal side. There's also a 5km (3 mile) walk along the sea wall, behind the beach heading west. The beach is well organised with areas marked for swimming and a boat-free zone. Lifeguards are on duty (30 min walk).

Le Grand Bunker, ave. du 6 Juin (25 min) provides deep immersion into the history of the Second World War. This blockhouse is built on five levels and was part of the German Atlantic Wall designed to prevent Allied attack. It has since been reconstructed, with ammunition, communications and officers' quarters. You get a complete view of the D-Day landing beaches from the roof.

Museum Commando No 4, Place Alfred Thomas (30 min) tells the story of the 177 French soldiers, all volunteers, in the Kieffer commando, and their part in the decisive Battle of Normandy.

FOOD AND SHOPPING

● **Intermarché** on the canal, western side (5 min walk).
● **Carrefour Market**, route de Caen (30 min walk).
● **Seafood market** (across the bridge) (10 min walk), **Carrefour Contact** a little further on rue Pasteur-Riva Bella (25 min walk).
● **Pharmacy, pizza** and **restaurants** close by the lock on the west side.
● Esplanade Alexandre Lofi – close by the beach on the western side of the harbour (30 min walk), where you'll find **cafés, restaurants** and a **casino.**

FURTHER AFIELD

Daily ferry connections with Portsmouth carry a million people a year. If visiting Caen, take a bus or train to Bayeaux to see the famous tapestry. The railway station in Caen, 14000 Caen, is on the Paris–Cherbourg line.

DIVES-SUR-MER

HONFLEUR 15NM, **LE HAVRE 13NM, ST VAAST 50NM**

The centre of this town is a jewel of medieval architecture. Most of the town is located to the south and west of the harbour, so walking is necessary.

NAVIGATION

A drying entrance leads to a well-built and well-equipped marina with 25 visitor berths, properly known as Port Guillaume. Deeper draft yachts need to enter approaching HW. You may be met and guided to your berth.

OVERVIEW

William the Conqueror set sail from here, but many harbours along this coast make that claim. However, above the church door you'll see engraved the names of his 475 companions, which gives Dives' claim some credibility.

This town was once home to a large steel plant, closed since the 1980s. The river cuts the marina off from the excellent beach, but there is a footbridge. The town on the northern side of the river is Cabourg, with Houlgate to the north-west.

THINGS TO SEE AND DO

Les Halles Médiévales de Dives-sur-Mer, rue Paul Canta (15 min walk) is a remarkable 14th-century market hall – a half-timbered building with a roof

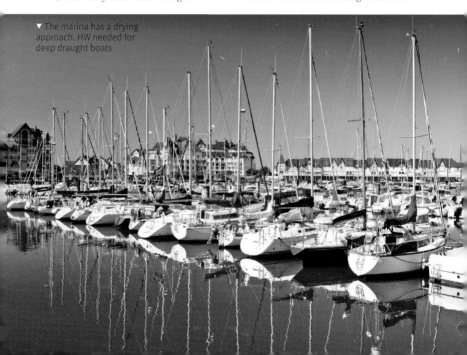

▼ The marina has a drying approach. HW needed for deep draught boats

The essentials:

FUEL On the marina. The marina office is the octagonal building by the lock on the south side of the marina.

REPAIRS/CHANDLERY On the marina – take advice from the harbour office. Lifting up to 30T (Travelift) can be arranged.

LAUNDRY In the marina, open all night.

CLUB The Société des Régates de Dives-Houlgate (SRDH) on the marina welcomes visitors.

HIRE Cycle hire at Dives Évasion, 14160 Dives-sur-Mer (15 min walk).

supported by 66 wooden pillars. It was built open-sided; the walls were added in the 20th century. Also in the market square is the substantial 17th-century stone-built manor house on five floors.

Close by is the **Village d'Art** (free entry), which portrays a typical Norman village and contains artisan shops – also tourist information (see below).

Within the harbour, look out for a small **fleet of traditional fishing boats**

from this area, made distinctive by their tan sails. These are proudly preserved by a team of volunteers.

If it's a blowy day and the family is bored try **Laser Quest**, rue de la Vignerie (30 min walk).

FOOD AND SHOPPING

- **Bakery** and **grocery** on the marina.
- **Carrefour Express**, 19 Place de la République (15 min walk).
- **Intermarché hypermarket**, ave. des Résistants (25 min walk).
- There is a weekly Saturday market in **Les Halles Médiévales** (see above), which overflows into the nearby streets.
- **Fish market** by the harbour, mornings all year round.

FURTHER AFIELD

There's an SNCF station at rue de l'Avenir (7 min) – trains to Deauville and connections to stations in northern France.

Tourist information
Village d'Art Guillaume-le-Conquérant (12 min), with reproduction of parts of the Bayeaux tapestry

▼ The beach is cut off from the marina by a river – but there's a footbridge

DEAUVILLE/ TROUVILLE

▲ Expect to find smart boats and smart people in Deauville

CHICHESTER 95NM, **CHERBOURG** 70NM, **FÉCAMP** 33NM

A pair of once very smart resorts either side of the Touques River, these towns are a touch less prosperous these days. The French first fell in love with sea bathing here in the 19th century and this place has been all about indulgence ever since. There's gambling, high fashion, horse racing and houses built to extravagant proportions. You'll need good walking shoes for exploring as the main marina is some way out of town.

NAVIGATION

The river and harbour entrance is dry, but with rise of tide and no strong onshore wind there's no problems here. Berthing is on the Deauville side amid modern development. The first marina to starboard is in Port Deauville, with the Bassin des Yachts and Bassin Morny further in, the latter two divided by a bridge. No berthing on the Trouville side. There is little hint of 'jet-set' lifestyle in either of these marinas and Port Deauville is further from the town than you might wish.

OVERVIEW

Napoleon III and his empress bestowed Trouville with its reputation through their frequent visits. The 1860s 'belle époque' feel the captain brought with him is said to linger here. Although you will berth in Deauville, of the two towns it is Trouville that has the feel of a 'real' place – the locals here aren't dependent on the annual Parisian tourists. The fine sand beach at Trouville is highly regarded and you'll find children's entertainment, bathing huts and food outlets aplenty. There is a lengthy promenade, which cuts off the town from the beach. On the far side, you'll see the famous majestic villas – a kind of mock-Tudor style that seems to have been popular – and you can't miss the casino.

Deauville, on the other hand, considers itself to be almost a suburb of Paris, more upmarket and distinctly

▲ Famous for its fish, you'll find plenty of top class restaurants in Deauville

more stylish. This is where you'll find the racecourse, which, together with the casino, offers many opportunities for a win (or loss!). This is also the major racehorse breeding area in France. Sir Winston Churchill tried his luck here, spending most of the

The essentials:

FUEL At Port Deauville, but beware moving around in the marina, which is laid out like a maze.

REPAIRS There is an 8T crane in the Bassin Morny. Or take advice from Deauville Nautisme, rue des Feugrais (15 min taxi ride out of town).

LAUNDRY At the marina, or the club (see below), or try Lavedeau S.A.R.L, 66 rue Victor Hugo (15 min walk).

CLUB Deauville Yacht Club, Quai de la Marine (15 min walk on the inner basin, the Bassin à Flot). The club was established in 1928 and is a major yachting centre where visitors are welcome. You'll find washing, toilet and shower facilities, but it's a bit of a hike from Port Deauville.

HIRE (On the Trouville side) Les Trouvillaises, 4 Place Foch (30 min walk).

FERRY From Deauville to Trouville, which can save you a lot of walking, but only when there is sufficient rise of tide. Leaves every five minutes from the Deauville side and lands you near the casino. You can cross via a pontoon bridge at LW.

SWIMMING Piscine Olympique de Deauville, blvd. de la Mer (6 min walk) or outdoor pool at Complexe Nautique du Front de Mer on the Trouville side, prom. des Planches (35 min walk).

summer of 1906 in the casino. The town was the brainchild of one Dr Olliffe who, in 1862, decided to create a 'town of pleasure' on what was once marsh and dunes. It is now known as the 'Queen of the Beaches' and is one of the smartest resorts in France (Yves Saint Laurent had a house here).

Trouville first achieved a reputation after the artist Charles Mozin painted the place in 1825, and it caught the eye of Proust, Dumas and Monet, among others.

THINGS TO SEE AND DO

Deauville

There is much pleasure to be had in wandering among the villas and gazing into the windows of very expensive boutiques, as well as enjoying the **1920s boardwalk** with its bathing cabins. The cabins are named after actors and directors who over the years have attended the annual American Film Festival held here.

Top polo players from the world come to play polo at the **Deauville International Polo Club**, blvd. Mauger (20 min walk). There's also racing on the flat and steeplechasing. They used to race on the beach before the **racecourse** was established (45 ave. Hocquart de Turtot (30 min walk).

Trouville

As in Deauville, there is much to be enjoyed by wandering among the wide range of architecture. The tourist info can arrange guided tours (in English). **Museé Villa Montebello**, 64 rue Général Leclerc, a grand mansion built in 1865, is now a municipal museum with paintings by Mozin.

You cannot avoid the imposing **casino** as you sail in, which has an array of slot machines, electronic games, poker, roulette, as well as bars and restaurants – it's an experience, even if you're not the gambling kind, Place Maréchal Foch (30 min walk).

▼ Shopping is good here, but expect to have to dig deep into your pocket

▲ Top class marina, but expect to do some walking

FOOD AND SHOPPING

● **Les 4 Marchands** (on Port Deauville) – well-stocked shop.

● **Carrefour Market**, 49 ave. de la République (20 min walk).

● **Deauville market** on Tuesday, Friday and Saturday mornings plus holidays and summer Sundays, Place du Marché (15 min walk).

● Trouville has a famous fish market, the **Marché aux Poissons**, 152 blvd. Fernand Moureaux (30 min walk). Originally built of wood and declared a historic monument, it was destroyed by fire in 2006 and later rebuilt as an exact replica.

● If eating out in style, try **Les Quatre Chats**, 8 rue d'Orléans (30 min walk) on the Trouville side for French food in a 1950s American diner setting. Matt Damon, Gwyneth Paltrow and George Lucas drop in when they're at the film festival. English is not spoken here. Expensive.

FURTHER AFIELD

The SNCF station is at Quai de la Gare (20 min walk) at the southern end of the Bassin à Flot. It's half-timbered as well. Trains, naturally, direct to Paris (2 hr 20 min).

Deauville Airport is 7km (4.3 miles) to the east of the town, 14130 St-Gatien-des-Bois (25 min by taxi). No scheduled flights but charter flights to all parts of Europe. Private jet charter is available.

There's a bus station close to the rail station (20 min walk).

Tourist information

Tourist Intercommunal Deauville, Quai de l'Impératrice Eugénie, near the railway station (15 min walk), or Office de Tourisme, Trouville, 32 blvd. Fernand Moureaux (20 min walk)

HONFLEUR

LE HAVRE 6NM, **FÉCAMP** 40NM, **OUISTREHAM** 18NM, **NAB TOWER** 90NM, **BRIGHTON** 85NM

There is no finer medieval harbour on the entire French coastline. It gets crowded in high summer but the sense of history is overwhelming – a real gem. You are now on the sandy Calvados Coast, which runs from here to the River Orne.

NAVIGATION

Honfleur is on the south bank of the Seine estuary and you approach by using the main channel, which runs between two training walls. Follow the buoyed channel with care. Be aware of a strong stream running across the harbour entrance. The lock (24 hr) opens on the hour inbound. Access to the Vieux Bassin – the pretty bit – requires passage through an opening bridge that has set opening times. Give way to departing yachts.

▼ The Lieutenance is one of two gates to the old town and home to the King's Lieutenant in the 17th century

OVERVIEW

Canada was colonised from here by those who set sail in 1608 to found the city of Quebec. Trade was conducted to Africa, the Azores and the West Indies. This was a major port for the trading of enslaved people.

Today, this is a town of cobbled streets, bustling bars, waterside restaurants and half-timbered houses, some so tall they look as though they might topple. Erik Satie, the composer and artist, was born here, and the impressionist painters Renoir, Cézanne and Pissarro loved it, as will you.

◀ The colourful timber-framed houses crowd the waterside of the old harbour

▶ St Catherine's Church built by shipwrights out of wood

THINGS TO SEE AND DO

You can't miss the **Lieutenance** as it sits over the inner harbour to the right as you come through the bridge, and is the former dwelling of the King's Lieutenant, acting as a gateway to the town.

St Catherine's Church, Place St Catherine, (very close to the harbour) is the grandest sight in Honfleur being built entirely of wood during the Hundred Years' War (1337–1453), when stone was required to build fortifications and so was diverted from churches. The church was built by shipwrights who had woodworking expertise.

Naturospace, blvd. Charles V (15 min walk north from the harbour) is a

tropical forest – on the Channel coast! Maintained at 27°C (80°F) all year round, within the glass house you'll find 1,000 butterflies and 350 botanical species. This is the best day out for families if the weather isn't to your liking.

Satie House Museum, 67 blvd. Charles V (10 min walk) is a somewhat surreal museum devoted to the composer – prepare for a mind-bending experience.

The Carousel is a fantastic traditional fairground ride outside the Mairie, Place de l'Hôtel de Ville (10 min walk) (May to October).

Honfleur Marine Museum, 11 Quai St-Etienne (3 min walk) on the eastern side of the inner basin is housed in the church of St Étienne. There's only one room but it has a good depiction of the maritime history of the town.

Butin Beach (Plage du Butin, blvd. Charles V, beyond the Naturospace, north of the harbour with café) has supervised swimming (be careful of the tides), showers, clean sand and a children's playground. A somewhat longish (25 min) walk if taking the roads. Instead, cut through the Parc des Impressionnistes for relief or via the Naturospace.

FOOD AND SHOPPING

- **Market** (supermarket), 46 rue de la République (10 min walk).
- **Market day** in Honfleur is Saturday, with stalls around the harbour.
- There is an **organic food market** Wednesday mornings at Place Sainte

▼ St Catherine's Church, the largest timber church in France. It dates from the second half of the 15th century.

▼ The most atmospheric of Normandy's harbours

Catherine (4 min walk).

● There's a huge tourist trade in all the **restaurants**, especially **close to the harbour**. Some have sacrificed quality in order to achieve the maximum throughput of customers. Choose with care.

● Claude Monet kept cookery notebooks and among his recipes was **chicken 'Honfleur' style**, which employed lots of butter, oil, Calvados and dry white wine. Make sure to try it while you're here.

FURTHER AFIELD

There is no train station, the nearest being at Pont-L'Évêque 20km (12.5 miles) to the south – bus service from there to Honfleur (No 50). The Gare Routiére (bus station), Rue des Vases, is to the east of the tourist information. There are several bus stops so check with tourist information first. Buses connect to all parts of France and wider Europe.

Tourist information

Quai Lepaulmier (10 min walk) – guided tours of the town start from here

▼ Honfleur is a hugely popular destination with its blend of atmosphere, history and best of Normandy food

THE NORMANDY AND PICARDY COAST

LE HAVRE ▶ DUNKERQUE

FROM LE HAVRE TO LE TREPORT, you are sailing the Côte d'Albâtre, or the Alabaster Coast. It includes Dieppe and St Valery en Caux, and if the dazzling white, chalky coastline looks familiar it is because it is the same geological formation as the White Cliffs of Dover.

The cliffs here are high and impressive and have been celebrated by impressionist painters including Monet, Pissarro and Renoir, who made art out of the contrasts between the whiteness of the cliffs and the blue/green of the Channel waters. You will find them equally inspiring (some cliffs

are as high as 120m/390ft), especially if you have come from the somewhat less dramatic Normandy beaches; less impressive, of course, in a geographical and not historical sense. Look out for the dry hanging valleys that are a feature of these cliffs. It is the most spectacular stretch of coastline at the eastern end of the Channel.

After Le Tréport, it is as if the coastline has given up, as its majestic cliffs start to fade into something more modest and industrialisation starts to overwhelm the charm. There are still attractive towns and beaches, but you are approaching Boulogne, Calais and eventually Dunkerque. Expect to see the towering chimneys of oil refineries, the to and fro of cross-Channel ferries and urgent fishing boats emerging from the port of Boulogne.

There is always good food to be had wherever you might be in France, and although this coastline might seem less inspiring than some other parts of the Channel, the food can be just as delicious as anything to be found elsewhere. For starters, try ficelle Picarde, crêpes filled with ham and grated cheese, and mushroom smothered in créme fraîche and baked. Rollot is common cheese round here. It is a soft cheese, usually heart-shaped, made from cow's milk. They produce champagne too in this part of France, making for a perfect ending to a Channel cruise.

▼ Normandy's answer to the white cliffs of Dover. The Alabaster beach has been an inspiration to some of France's greatest painters

LE HAVRE

NAB TOWER 85NM, **BRIGHTON** 80NM, **FÉCAMP** 25NM, **HONFLEUR** 11NM

This is the second largest port in France (after Marseille) at the mouth of the River Seine and a busy commercial harbour. There's a very clean 2km (1.3 mile)-long shingle beach with a vibrant promenade. Much modern building surrounds the large marina area.

NAVIGATION

You can arrive in all weathers, at all states of tide, and get good shelter. The two marinas are found by turning sharp left once you are through the harbour entrance. A glance at the chart reveals the substantial number of buoys in the major ship channel and at night this can appear like Christmas illuminations. Yachts are not allowed to use this approach channel.

OVERVIEW

The harbour was occupied by German forces in 1940 when they set up fortifications with orders that the city was to be defended till the last man was standing. Consequently, it endured 132 bombings, and one raid by Britain's Royal Air Force wiped out most of the downtown area, making it one of the most destroyed European towns of the war – more than 12,000 buildings were lost. Rather than reconstructing, as many towns and cities chose to do, Le Havre (trans: 'the harbour') was rebuilt in a modernist style that for traditional

The essentials:

FUEL Diesel berth in the south corner of the Anse de Joinville.

REPAIRS, chandlery, facilities, laundry and engineers available in this large marina complex – ask at the harbour office. Sailmaker – All Purpose Le Havre, 23 rue Auguste Constant Guerrier (10 min walk).

CLUBS The Société Nautique du Havre, Quai Eric Tabarly (4 min walk) is a convivial and welcoming place. The Société des Régates du Havre (close to the above) is the oldest club in continental Europe. A more formal dining experience.

HIRE There are several cycle hires: try Giant Le Havre, 3 Quai Casimir Delavigne (20 min) or Citibike, 9 rue Jules Siegfried (15 min).

SWIMMING Piscine Municipal Le Havre (indoor), 37 Cours de la République (30 min) or Club Nautique Le Havre (outdoor swimming in sea water), blvd. Clemenceau (5 min north of the marina).

Note: the harbour office can be found at the head of the walls that divide the marinas. You'll also find some tourist information here.

▲ Le Havre marina at night

tastes, makes it less beguiling than some other French harbours. However, lovers of modern architecture, and especially reinforced concrete, will want to seek out this city, which is on the UNESCO World Heritage Site list. The architect in charge of the entire post-war reconstruction was Auguste Perret, who declared 'concrete is beautiful'. You will have time to consider this while enjoying the views from the marina.

It is often remarked upon that the city has a sense of space, with the skyline kept deliberately low and green spaces and sea views incorporated into its development. The marina is close to both the beach and the downtown district. The harbour was once an important connection with the Americas, being both a terminal for Atlantic passenger liners and an import base for coffee and cotton, as well as wine and oil from the Mediterranean.

THINGS TO SEE AND DO

St Joseph's Church, 130 blvd. François, (5 min) is remarkable. A neo-gothic temple built of reinforced concrete, its architect proved that concrete could support a 100m (328ft) tower. You will doubtless see this from a distance as you navigate your way into the harbour.

Musée d'Art Moderne André Malraux, close to the marina, 2 blvd. Clemenceau (10 min), houses five centuries of art in a modern gallery, reflecting the well-known artists who came to this area to paint – Monet and Renoir among them.

Espace Oscar-Niemeyer-Le Volcan, 8 Place Oscar Niemeyer (15 min), known as the 'volcano' or sometimes the 'yoghurt pot', is a cultural centre by the designer of Brasilia and the UN building in New York City. You'll find

▲ Rich grazing produces fine milk for the best camembert cheeses – baguette not optional

theatre, music and dance here.

If you want to escape the modernist architecture try **Le Havre Cathedral**, rue de Paris (15 min), built in the late 1500s although only declared a cathedral in 1974. It has an organ donated by Cardinal Richelieu.

Quartier St-Vincent is the one part of the city that survived the war and sits between the rebuilt city centre and the beach. It's notable for the church of **St Vincent de Paul**, 14 Place St Vincent de Paul (15 min).

FOOD AND SHOPPING

● **Market day** every day (0830–2130). Sunday morning only **Halles Centrales**, rue Bernardin de St Pierre.
● **Super U et Drive** (well stocked), 5 rue Abbé Périer (6 min).
● **U Express**, Place des Halles Centrales (10 min).
● Look out for regional cheeses, among them **Camembert**, **Neufchâtel** and **Pont l'Evêque**.

FURTHER AFIELD

The SNCF station is at 12 rue Magellan (30 min walk) – trains to Paris (2 hr 30 min) and all cities in northern France.

Portsmouth to Le Havre is operated by Brittany Ferries (5.5 hr). The ferry port is located at Terminal de la Citadelle (25 min walk).

Buses to all parts of France from Terminal de la Citadelle (25 min – close to the ferry terminal).

> **Tourist information**
> 186 blvd. Clémenceau (4 min walk north from the marina office)

FÉCAMP

ST VALERY EN CAUX 17NM, **DIEPPE** 32NM, **LE HAVRE** 25NM,
CHERBOURG 78NM, **BRIGHTON** 70NM

There is much history here in what was once France's major cod fishing port, set among some of the tallest cliffs in Normandy.

NAVIGATION

Moderate onshore winds create a run of surf that can make for a difficult entrance, otherwise it is free of dangers. There's good shelter once inside, although L'Avant Port may feel the swell in onshore winds.

OVERVIEW

Fishing has always been the basis of Fécamp's prosperity, from the 10th century when it was salted herrings, to whaling and eventually cod. It was once France's premier port for cod fishing, which collapsed after the Canadians refused the French access to their cod grounds in the 1970s.

Bénédictine, a herbal liqueur flavoured with berries, herbs and spices, was made from a recipe taken from the Benedictine monks from the abbey at Fécamp. The recipe was destroyed in the French revolution but, conveniently, was rediscovered in the 19th century. You can believe this if you wish – the drink is somewhat easier to swallow.

▼ Fécamp – protected by the high cliffs of Normandy

THINGS TO SEE AND DO

There is history aplenty here. The **Bénédictine Palace Museum**, 110 rue Alexandre le Grand, (12 min walk) is more of a Gothic palace than a museum, built to honour the famous drink. There's also a distillery with a collection of religious and modern art.

You won't keep the kids away from **Musée du chocolat & Boutique Hautot**, 851 rte de Valmont (45 min walk) where you will find games, activities and, of course, much chocolate-tasting. It's an hour's walk inland, so a taxi ride is 15 min.

Musée des Pêcheries, 3 Quai Capitaine Jean Recher (10 min walk) is a new museum in a former cod-drying factory. Fishing and fine arts sit side by side, and there are spectacular views from the roof of the museum.

The **Boucane Du Grand Quai**, 16 Grand Quai (10 min walk) is where herrings were gutted, smoked and boxed. It has hosted guided tours since its closure as a factory in 1996.

Patrimoine Visites Blockhaus (a stiff uphill walk of 30 min), high on the cliffs on the northern side of the harbour, close to Cap Fagnet overlooking the sea, is part of a guided tour of wartime relics including what is believed to be a German military hospital carved into the chalk. It's an intriguing place, which kids seem to enjoy exploring. Open Wednesday and Saturday – ask at the tourist information (below).

▼ Once the home of a huge cod fishing fleet, pleasure boats are now the main customers

▼ The Bénédictine Palace in Fécamp

The **Ducal Palace**, 1–3 Rue André Paul Leroux (25 min walk) was built between the 10th and 12th centuries for the first Duke of Normandy. William the Conqueror came here in 1067 to celebrate victory at Hastings. Access only with a guide.

FOOD AND SHOPPING

- There's plenty of food shopping to be had close to the **marina**.
- **Carrefour City**, 83–85 Quai Berigny (10 min walk).
- For a larger shop, try **Carrefour Fécamp**, rue Charles Leborgne (20 min walk).
- **Intermarché SUPER**, 79–83 rue Queue de Renard (30 min walk). **Aldi** is close by.
- The **fish market** opens Friday and Saturday mornings. As well as fish there's **local cheese**, **veg** and the **all-important cider**.

FURTHER AFIELD

The SNCF rail station is a 15 min walk from the marina at blvd. de la République. Good connections to the ferry port at Le Havre to facilitate crew changes. Buses operate from the rail station. Ficibus is part of the Fécamp public transport system and is mainly for local journeys.

Tourist information
Quai Sadi Carnot (12 min walk on the far side of the inner basin, Bassin Bérigny)

▼ The Fécamp fishing fleet much reduced these days

ST VALERY EN CAUX

DIEPPE 20NM, BOULOGNE 60NM, BRIGHTON 70NM, FÉCAMP 20NM

This is a small but friendly town, rebuilt after the war – a popular resort in a compact setting.

NAVIGATION

A drying entrance with outer breakwaters – be careful of the cross stream here and approach after half tide. There is one pair of lock gates and a lifting bridge, but waiting buoys are provided. Once inside the inner harbour, you'll be glad you made the effort.

OVERVIEW

This is a charming and friendly town, severely damaged during the Second World War and since rebuilt. It was here in 1940 that the British surrendered to Rommel, and it wasn't until late 1944 that the town was liberated.

The high chalk cliffs continue to be the theme of the landscape. There's a pebble beach, with clean sand at low tide. This friendly little town was once home to a busy herring fleet but is now largely the domain of tourists.

THINGS TO SEE AND DO

Try the **casino**, 1 prom. Jacques Couture (10 min walk) for gambling, music, cocktails, food, cinema and a hotel, all overlooking the sea.

The covered **Littoral Swimming Pool**, 26 rue Hochet (20 min south of the marina) has pools for both serious swimmers and children.

▼ A very welcoming harbour

The **Henri IV Museum**, Quai d'Aval, is a timber-framed house built in 1540 and features local history. This is also the tourist information (2 min walk, close by the lock gates).

▲ A 16th-century house, named Henri IV. Now a local history museum

FOOD AND SHOPPING

● **E. Leclerc hypermarket**, 11 ave. de la 51e Highland Division (25 min walk out of town to industrial estate). Taxi recommended.

● Across the bridge to **Carrefour Express**, 3 rue des Remparts (4 min walk).

● **Market day** is Friday, with a Sunday market in the tourist season.

● The **annual Mackerel Festival** is held in July, and in August the **Festival of the Sea**. On the third Sunday in November, the **herring** is celebrated, and eaten, with gusto.

● **Restaurant du Port**, 18 Quai d'Amont (across the bridge, 5 min walk) for everything fish, but perhaps not with small children (no kids' menu). The **mussels** here are remarkable. Opposite, the **local fishing boats** tie up to sell their catch direct.

The essentials:

FUEL None on the marina but a nearby service station.

REPAIRS Mobile cranes can lift up to 10T – there's a chandlery at Accastillage Diffusion, close by the marina.

FACILITIES At the yacht club building, by the marina.

LAUNDRY Close by the marina or Laverie Libre Service, 26 Place de la Chapelle (across the bridge, 6 min walk).

FURTHER AFIELD

There is no train station here (closed in the 1990s). Five buses a day run between Dieppe to St Valery en Caux if you were changing crews with the UK or needed to return home. Few buses at weekends.

Tourist information
In the Henri IV museum, close to the marina lock gates (2 min walk)

DIEPPE

▲ Enter this marina at any state of tide

LE TRÉPORT 15NM, **ST VALERY EN CAUX** 16NM, **FÉCAMP** 30NM, **BRIGHTON** 72NM, **LE HAVRE** 55NM

You'll find a good atmosphere, good facilities and easy navigation in this city.

NAVIGATION

An easy harbour to enter and plenty of water. A call must be made on VHF12 3.2km (2 miles) out and before leaving. The marina can be entered at any state of tide – no locks.

OVERVIEW

This is a vibrant French city and you can moor in the highly rated Port de Plaisance Jehan Ango, close to the heart of the city. Step off your boat, cross the road and there are enough dining and shopping opportunities to last at least a week. The beach is shingle, and can be steep.

Apart from its strategic position – which William the Conqueror made use of in preparation for his invasion in 1066 – the city gained notoriety in the 16th century due to its school of cartography, which produced some of France's most celebrated navigators. One of the town's most famous

The essentials:

FUEL Diesel and petrol available 24 hr with a credit/debit card. There is a wave-break protecting the marina as you enter and the fuel berth is on the quayside, tucked behind it.

REPAIRS The marina has lifting, launching and hard-standing facilities. A group of engineers and shipwrights work under the banner of 'Dieppe Navals' and can help with all maintenance issues.

LAUNDRY Close to the marina, ask at harbour office, or Lav-O-Clair, 19 rue Notre Dame (6 min walk).

CLUB The Dieppe Yacht Club, Quai du Carénage, can be found on the first floor of the Ango building, which also houses the marina office. Visitors are welcome. The marina office is at the southern end of the marina.

residents, Jehan Ango (after whom the marina is named) provided ships for French global expeditions, intending to rival the Spanish and Portuguese. Merchants brought spices from the east, including cinnamon, which was embraced as a flavouring for pudding rice baked with cream to create the still popular teurgoule.

The harbour was used as an embarkation point for emigrants bound for Canada, where there is another 'Dieppe'. It has been a wartime target since 1694, when the Anglo-Dutch bombarded it, but its darkest moment was the Dieppe raid of August 1942, an invasion attempt described as a 'fiasco' that left thousands of young soldiers (mostly Canadians) dead on the beach.

The town has always been popular with British artists and literary figures – JMW Turner visited here. It eventually became popular as a resort for Parisian families on lower incomes in the middle of the 20th century.

THINGS TO SEE AND DO

Cité de la Mer, 37 rue de l'Asile Thomas (5 min walk north from the marina towards the harbour mouth) is a museum blending science research with fun for kids. It tells the story of seafaring, from Norman times to the present day. Hands-on radio-controlled boats keep the family happy.

The **Château-Musée**, rue de Chastes (15 min walk) gives a wider picture of the history of Dieppe, and has been housed in the castle since 1923. There are 15 rooms of exhibits, including impressionist paintings.

Catch the **International Dieppe Kite Festival** if you are here in early September.

Les Bains de Dieppe, 101 blvd. de Verdun (15 min walk, behind the beach west of the harbour mouth) has swimming, a whirlpool, a paddling pool, water games, and a restaurant with the Channel view. It's a top place for a weather-bound family.

FOOD AND SHOPPING

- **Carrefour City** is close by the marina, 22 Quai Duquesne (5 min walk beyond the harbour office) or **Vival** (modest), 2 bis rue Duquesne (5 min walk)
- Voted the **best French market** in 2020, the market runs every Saturday morning and is busy from opening time at 0800. Expect over 200 stalls. It is the largest in Normandy and is found on the road that runs straight past the marina. Here you will discover **lisettes** (baby mackerel) and **gendarmes** (smoked herrings) – both local specialities.

▼ The Château-Musée with the history of Dieppe

FURTHER AFIELD

The train station no longer has direct services to Paris and other cities in northern France. Take the train to Rouen and make connections there. DFDS ferries offers two ferries from Dieppe to Newhaven on Transmanche Ferries (4 hr crossing). Timetables can vary due to tidal restrictions.

Tourist information
Pont Jehan Ango, a glass-walled block on the bridge at the western end of the marina (5 min walk)

▲ Dieppe's kite festival, every two years usually in September   ▶ The market in Dieppe has been voted 'best French market'

LE TRÉPORT

▶ A locked marina
with strong cross tides
in the entrance

ST VALERY SUR SOMME 15NM, **ÉTAPLES** 30M, **DIEPPE** 14NM,
EASTBOURNE 60NM

This is a fishing town and a working harbour where the River Bresle meets the sea. At Mers-les-Bains, to the north, is the once-fashionable bathing beach (pebbles and sand) complete with architecture from the belle époque. It was a favourite haunt of Parisian tourists in the 19th century due to the direct rail line from Le Tréport to Paris.

NAVIGATION

The entrance dries at LW but can be recognised by the gap in the tall white cliffs. Once through the entrance, head for the southernmost lock, which leads to the marina with 20 visitor berths. There are strong cross currents between the pier heads. If manoeuvring prior to going through the locks, the outer harbour can be shallow away from the Channel.

OVERVIEW

You are now at one end of the Alabaster Coast (famously painted by Claude Monet), which runs from here to Le Havre and is notable for its cliffs that rise up to 120m (390ft), making them the highest chalk cliffs in Europe. They are illuminated at night, which might aid navigation.

▼ Le Tréport shelters under the tall Normandy cliffs – there's a funicular railway to the top

You will find more pebbles than sand on the beaches. This was a Viking landing place in the 10th century. The town was badly damaged in the Second World War and was awarded the Croix de Guerre, given for acts of heroism in conflicts.

THINGS TO SEE AND DO

The **Funicular Railway**, rue Amiral Courbet (14 min walk) takes you from the town to the cliff top, and it's free! There's also a tourist information centre at the top, rue du Télécabine.

The town's museum, **Musée du Vieux Tréport**, 1 rue de l Anguainerie (10 min walk) is modest and won't detain you for more than an hour, but it gives a good insight into the largely maritime history.

There is kayaking, wind surfing

The essentials:

FUEL No fuel at the marina. Ask for latest advice on availability of diesel – you may have to carry it in cans.

FACILITIES On the marina.

REPAIRS There is a crane at the Yacht Club de la Bresle, 1 Quai des Paquebots, but limited to 6T. You may be able to get engineering advice here but they appear to be geared only for servicing small fishing boats. Also a chandlery.

LAUNDRY There is no laundry at the marina. Try Aqu@net, 4 rue du Duc de Penthièvre (12 min walk).

HIRE Cycles at Magasin Boutique Vanille in Mers-les-Bains, 19 rue Buzeaux (25 min walk or a 5 min taxi ride).

▼ A once fashionable beach in this town which is nice blend of resort and working harbour

and paddle boarding at various watersports clubs in town. Consult tourist information for those that are operating during your visit.

Annual **sea festivals** are common along this stretch of coast and almost every maritime community has a yearly celebration.

The **Herring Festival** starts in Le Tréport and moves along the coast to Dieppe in November. The herrings here are known as the 'king of fish'. You can eat your fill in the streets to musical accompaniment.

Every two years, Le Tréport has its own **Sea Festival** in July, when children and grandchildren of fishermen carry boxes of wheat and salt; the fishing fleet puts to sea to gather for a Mass and Blessing.

FOOD AND SHOPPING

● The small fishmarket, **Marché aux Poissons**, caters to every fishy appetite and is open every day, Place de la Poissonnerie (12 min walk towards the harbour mouth).

● For the nearest supermarket, try the small but friendly **Carrefour Contact**, 1 ave. des Canadiens (5 min walk).

● For stocking up, head for **Intermarche SUPER hypermarket**, ZAC Les Prés Salés. Take a taxi (10 min) or walk (50 min – not recommended). There is an **Aldi** close by.

FURTHER AFIELD

The SNCF train station is in Mers Le Bains on the far side of the river, Place Pierre Sémard (15 min walk north from the marina) with trains to all parts of the coast and Paris (approx. 4 hr). There is a bus service to Dieppe (45 min).

Tourist information
Very close to the marina, where every help is offered, blvd. du Calvaire (2 min walk)

ST VALERY SUR SOMME

BOULOGNE 30NM, **FOLKESTONE** 54NM, **EASTBOURNE** 60NM,
LE HAVRE 75NM

This quiet and attractive town is beloved by holidaymakers. Pity about the tricky entrance.

NAVIGATION

The entrance to the River Somme crosses extensive drying sandbanks and the route meanders to the extent that navigation can be testing. Depths are limited, even at HW, and beware strong cross tides when approaching the marina. It's an ideal place for the experienced navigator blessed with a shallow draft boat, but not for the nervous. Your reward is a delightful

▼ If you make it this far, you've done well – a tricky entrance

medieval town and shelter from all weathers. There are 30 visitor berths in the marina.

OVERVIEW

This was where William the Conqueror brought together his fleet for his planned assault on England in 1066. Joan of Arc was held here by the English in 1431 before being burned at the stake, and her cell can still be seen. The ancient spirit of this town survives and this is a charming place to spend a few days. With its traditional red brick houses with city walls, cobbled streets, and abundant use of flowers as civic decoration, this is the sort of place you'd be happy to be storm-bound.

The essentials:

FUEL No diesel on the marina but a filling station reasonably close by (500m/0.3 miles).

REPAIRS You'll have to pass via a lock into the Canal de la Somme, where you will find a boatyard.

CHANDLERY Near the club.

FACILITIES Laundry and showers at the Sport Nautique Valericain, which is the yacht club on the marina.

HIRE Cycle hire at Quai Jules Verne (30 min walk – you have to cross the canal).

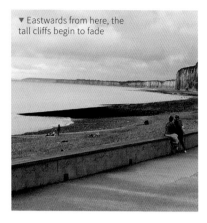

▼ Eastwards from here, the tall cliffs begin to fade

THINGS TO SEE AND DO

A lengthy and attractive **promenade** (3.5km/2.2 miles) runs alongside the river, making it a simple walk from the marina to the white sand beach at the northern end of the town, although a 35 min walk. There's **mini golf** along the way if you want to break up your walk. Note that if you're swimming, there can be strong currents off this beach.

For a relaxing and scented walk, try the **City Wall Herbarium** (20 min walk). This is a small herb and rare vegetable garden within the walls, once tended by nuns from the hospital and now used by local chefs to add individuality to their dishes.

Canoe and kayak tours run from Pilgrim Guide Baie de Somme at Chaussée du Cap Hornu, close by the beach. Expect to see seals – one of the largest seal colonies on this coast is hereabouts.

For a 3 hr **guided walking tour of the estuary** (in English, minimum five people) with a naturalist, contact enbaieaveclucas@gmail.com.

The **Somme Bay narrow gauge railway** provides vintage steam travel in genuine belle époque carriages between Le Crotoy and Cayeux-sur-Mer via St Valery. Call +33 (0)3 22 26 96 96.

The **Museé Picarvie**, 5 Quai du Romerel (15 min walk north from the marina) recreates a 19th-century Picardy

◄ The marina sits close to a charming medieval town

village complete with blacksmiths, shops, school and linen workshops, once an important industry in this region. There's plenty here to occupy families or crews of all ages.

FOOD AND SHOPPING

- The nearest supermarket is **Intermarché SUPER**, rue Caveé l'Évêque (10 min walk SW from the marina). There's a **McDonald's** a little further along the main road.
- **Local lamb** is highly prized for its delicate flavour imparted by the rich variety of grasses and herbs the lambs consume as they graze the salt marshes of the estuary – seek it out.
- Try the **Boucherie M.et Mme Deneux**, 35 rue de la Ferté (10 min walk north along the river bank) – an excellent shopping street with **bakeries**, **cafés** and **restaurants**.
- Try **Picardy beaten cake**, a tall, cylindrical cake, a bit like a brioche and very rich. You may find it as **gâteau battu** and it is recommended to be eaten with rhubarb jam.
- There is a **food market** by the riverside on Wednesday and Sunday morning.
- For **fish** – **Le Mathurin**, a family-owned restaurant with fresh fish counter alongside at 1 Place des Pilotes (15 min walk north from the marina along the promenade). Seek out the **scallops** and **samphire**, locally harvested. It's a smart place, despite the lack of tablecloths. Not cheap but very satisfying.

FURTHER AFIELD

The nearest SNCF station is in Noyelles-sur-Mer (15 min bus ride, 80 min walk). Bus route LR80706 for Noyelles-sur-Mer. Bus station outside the railway terminus, Place de la Gare, close by the marina. Train connections to all parts of northern France from there.

Tourist information
2 Place Guillaume le Conquérant
(7 min walk)

▼ It's safe and secure – once you're in!

ÉTAPLES

▲ A drying marina, so bilge keelers will be happiest here

BOULOGNE-SUR-MER 13NM, **ST VALERY EN CAUX** 17NM, **EASTBOURNE** 50NM, **DIEPPE** 40NM

Full of charm, this is a quiet town with some spirit about it, to be found at the mouth of the River Canche. It is marked in some books as Le Touquet, which is its (faded) neighbour on the other bank of the river. A drying marina.

NAVIGATION

Very shallow entrance that dries up to 3.2km (2 miles) offshore with a drying marina, so suited only to shallow draft boats that can take the ground. The tide runs strongly through the marina. Be warned – there is a low bridge close ahead of the marina.

OVERVIEW

Everyone from Julius Caesar to Napoleon as well as the British in the First World War used this town as a military base. In the 1980s, two-thirds of its population were seafaring families, but the increase in the size of fishing boats coupled with silting and shifts in the River Canche forced parts of the fleet to operate from Boulogne. However, there is plenty of fish to be had here and the 12 stalls in the fish market will fulfil all your fishy desires. Buy direct from fishermen here.

Artists have been drawn to this town by the quality of the light and in the early 20th century this was the home of an important school of artists, highly regarded and producing some fine maritime work.

THINGS TO SEE AND DO

There are two **maritime museums**: La Marine and Maréis – visit them in that order. Musée de la Marine, blvd. de l'Imperatrice (very close to the marina) covers the fishing history of the last century, complete with a visit to *Saint Josse*, an old Étaples trawler. Museum-Aquarium Maréis, blvd. Bigot Descelers (5 min walk) describes itself as a 'Sea Fishing Discovery Centre' and is dedicated to the work of modern fishermen. There's the wheelhouse of a modern vessel and a tactile aquarium, which allows young hands to dabble in the water. Guided tours take 1 hr.

Traditional wooden shipbuilding, blvd. Bigot Descelers (5 min walk) is the place to see boatbuilding construction using traditional skills and methods. This is as much a museum as a working boatyard so you'll see a huge range of vessels from traditional craft to modern repairs.

There are over 11,000 graves in the First World War cemetery to the north

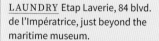

The essentials:

REPAIRS Boatyard and chandlery by the marina.

LAUNDRY Etap Laverie, 84 blvd. de l'Impératrice, just beyond the maritime museum.

SHOPPING Carrefour City is on the roundabout at the end of the bridge, just above the marina. Pharmacy next door. Nicolas wine shop, also on this roundabout, with a boulangerie and patisserie next door.

▼ A First World War memorial with 11,000 graves

of the town on the road to Boulogne
– it's breathtaking in its size, and
remarkable for its peace and
tranquillity. The monument is the
work of Sir Edward Lutyens.

Tourist information
La Corderie, short walk NW from
the marina

FOOD AND SHOPPING

● **Market** Tuesday and Friday.
● **Aux Pêcheurs d'Éataples**, blvd. de
l'Imperatrice, close to the marina (5 min
walk) is set above the fish market and
serves some of the **finest fish dishes of
northern France** – not the cheapest place
to eat, though. Try the **shop** on the
ground floor if you are cooking on board.

FURTHER AFIELD

The SNCF rail station, Étaples le
Touquet, is in the centre of town, Place
de la Gare (10 min walk) with trains
to Calais (1 hr) for crew changes. Bus
services also operate to Calais – check
with the marina office for the nearest
bus stop.

BOULOGNE-SUR-MER

CALAIS 22NM, **DOVER** 25NM, **EASTBOURNE** 48NM, **ÉTAPLES** 13NM

There's much history and atmosphere in the old town, but no longer any cross-Channel ferry traffic. It still has one of the largest fishing fleets in France and is home to the largest aquarium in Europe.

NAVIGATION

No dangers in the entrance, which is protected by large breakwaters, parts of the northern one being submerged. There are two marinas: L'Avant Port is accessible at all states of tide, and there is a locked marina in the Bassin Napoléon. Ignore the furthest locked marina, which is for small local boats. This is a hard-working and, occasionally, fishy-smelling harbour. Expect plenty of traffic.

OVERVIEW

Properly known as Boulogne-Sur-Mer, the harbour was founded by Julius Ceasar, who had his eyes on that country on the far side of the Channel. Atop the old Roman walls you'll find arguably the finest fortified 13th-century medieval town in France.

▼ Fishing boats and pleasure craft live side by side in Boulogne

The essentials:

FUEL At the marina but only −3 to +3 hr either side of HW, but cans can be filled at any time.

REPAIRS 35T Travelift at the marina.

LAUNDRY Two washing machines and two dryers at the marina.

HIRE At Cycléco, Pont Marguet (3 min walk from marina).

Forget the rest of this city, which lost much of its heart with the decline of the ferry traffic, and head for the old part. There are four gates to the walled part of town and you'll find information at the western one, Portes des Dunes (25 min walk).

Within the walls, and within the 13th-century castle is the **Château-Musée de Boulogne-Sur-Mer**, 1 Rue de Bernet, an art museum with a reputation for its collection of Egyptian artefacts rivalling the British Museum's collection. The **Basilique Notre-Dame**, 2 Parvis Notre Dame, stands proudly over the town, modelled on St Peter's in Rome and St Paul's in London. The walkways on top of the old walls give splendid views over the town and sea.

THINGS TO SEE AND DO

There is enough within the walled city to occupy you for a full day. But, especially for children and lovers of the sea, the **Nausicaà**, blvd. St-Beuve on the coast, north of the harbour (30 min walk) is the French National Sea Experience, the largest aquarium in Europe, housing 1,000 species and complete with penguins, sea lions and sharks. All signage here is in English as well as French. Open 0930–1830 every day – tickets can be bought online in advance to save waiting time. While there, you can easily make a full day of it by enjoying the splendid beach, the **Plage de Boulogne**, which fronts it.

On your way from your boat, you might want to pause at the 'Shaking Hands' monument, Quai Gambetta (20 min walk), unveiled in 2004 to depict the enduring friendship between France and the UK, just in case you were in any doubt.

The **House of Beurière**, 16 rue du Machicoulis (20 min walk north of the harbour) is for those who want to enjoy the real maritime history of Boulogne. Le Beurière was the name of the fishermen's quarter and this museum, which

◀ The largest aquarium in Europe – you can easily spend a full day here

▼ The Basilica of Notre
Dame, Boulogne

▼ A Viking ship, recently built, beneath the city walls

takes the form of a preserved house, gives you a real sense of a fisherman's lifestyle in the days when the Boulogne fleets sailed for Iceland and Newfoundland.

There's also a **casino** close to the south end of the marina.

FOOD AND SHOPPING

● **Carrefour Market** Boulogne-Sur-Mer Liane, 17 blvd. Daunou (10 min walk)
● The **fish market**, which opens 0630–1230, is a fish-lover's dream come true,

as it should be in France's premier fishing port. Take a fishy reference book with you as there will surely be fish here you won't recognise. On Sundays there is a **fruit and veg market** alongside.
● The **town market** on Wednesday and Saturday, held in the Place Dalton, can make for good morning's shopping (15 min walk).

FURTHER AFIELD

If needing to return to the UK for a crew change, take the train to Calais and connect with the ferries there (30 min by car) or to Lille (1 hr by car) to join the Eurostar. The train station, Gare de Boulogne-Ville, is at 3 blvd. Voltaire (30 min walk).

Tourist information
30 rue de la Lampe (12 min walk)

▼ More peaceful in the harbour now the ferry traffic has left

CALAIS

This is the major ferry port on the French Channel coast with 10 million passengers a year passing through, but it's also a useful city for cruisers with children, well catered for by miles of clean sandy beaches.

NAVIGATION

Easily spotted from sea by the white octagonal lighthouse with black lantern room atop. To find the harbour mouth you can spot the near continuous stream of ferries. Be cautious of the off-lying sandbanks, and cross tides across the entrance, which might run at 3 knots. If possible, time your arrival to suit lock opening times; this gives you access to the marina. If you miss the lock, there are waiting buoys, but these can provide a lumpy ride. The surroundings are not terribly inspiring.

OVERVIEW

Calais is the principal French Channel ferry port and lies on the 'Opal Coast' of France, which consists of 160km (100 miles) of sandy beaches, dunes, cliffs and resorts. Between here and Boulogne is the 'Great Site of the Two Capes', Cap Blanc-Nez and Cap Gris-Nez (White Nose and Grey Nose), with spectacular hiking atop the cliffs.

Calais has been a major trading hub since the Middle Ages, and was captured by the English in 1347 and remained in their hands until 1558. It was a major target for German forces in the Second World War, who built rocket launching sites along the nearby coast, trained on England. During the fierce battles for the city the entire place was more or less flattened. The Siege of Calais in 1940 took place shortly before the famous evacuation of British troops

The essentials:

FUEL Self-service at the marina is 24 hr. Also unleaded petrol – card payment required.

REPAIRS Scrubbing grid or lift-out for major repairs.

CHANDLERY From Calais Nautic in the Bassin Ouest, but with unusual opening hours so check before walking there.

FACILITIES Toilet facilities are of a high standard.

LAUNDRY There were machines on the marina, otherwise Laverie Automatique, 48 Place d'Armes (15 min walk).

CLUB The Bar du Yacht club and Le Yachting Club (good for cocktails) are close to the marina office.

HIRE Vel'In is a self-service bike hire system and there are 38 pick-up points within Calais. The network is run by Calais Opale Bus.

2

3

4

from the beaches off Dunkerque.

What is called the 'old town' lies on an artificially created island, with water on all sides – almost. It is an easy walk from the marina but don't expect too much antiquity – much of that was lost in the war.

THINGS TO SEE AND DO

This is a lace-making part of France, celebrated in the **Cité de la Dentelle et de la Mode** at 135 Quai du Commerce – the lace and textile museum (30 min walk).

The **Musée des Beaux-Arts**, the museum of fine arts, 25 rue Richelieu (20 min walk) is housed in an inspiring open space and offers workshops for children. English is spoken.

Lovers of **beaches** will gasp at the miles of clean sand. The closet beach to the marina can be found by simply heading northwards towards the main harbour entrance. There are ample food and drink opportunities along this stretch of beach but they can be well spaced out.

FOOD AND SHOPPING

● **Match Supermarket** (modest) on the Place d'Armes is the nearest to the marina (12 min walk).
● **Aldi** at 93 rue de Verdun (20 min walk) or 110 rue Mollien (30 min walk).
● Not forgetting **Majestic Wine Calais**, 3a ave. Charles de Gaulle (10 min by taxi).
● **Hypermarkets** are in the industrial areas of the city, so call a taxi.
● **Market days** are on Wednesday at the **Place d'Armes** (15 min walk) and Thursday at **Place Crèvecoeur** in the St Pierre district (40 min walk or 10 min by taxi). Both markets are open Saturdays as well.
● The nearest bakery is **Boulangerie Fred** (stunning bread and pastries), 120 blvd. Jacquard (25 min walk).

FURTHER AFIELD

A major ferry port with regular sailings. There are 88 Channel crossings a day – P&O and DFDS are the major operators sailing to Dover and Folkestone. If leaving a boat, there is a regular bus service to the ferry port from the SNCF station.

The SNCF station is called Calais-Ville, 46, ave. du Président Wilson (30 min walk). Although a main railway hub, this is a modest and less than comfortable station.

The Calais Centre Ville bus station is at 17 Quai du Rhin, close to the SNCF station. A bus ticket to Paris can be bought for 12 euros (2020) but it's a but it's a 5 hr journey.

For local buses, the Calais Opale Bus offers a free shuttle service around Calais, Monday to Saturday 0900–1900. The nearest stop to the marina is at the Place d'Armes.

The nearest French airport to Calais is in Lille, 112km (70 miles) away.

Tourist information
12 blvd. Georges Clemenceau
(20 min walk)

◀ **1** Many useful landmarks when making landfall off Calais; **2** Not just a ferry port but a resort as well with excellent beaches; **3** Good security behind the lock gates in Calais; **4** Much rebuilt after the Second World War, Calais is now a major commercial centre

GRAVELINES

RAMSGATE 33NM, **DOVER** 32NM, **DUNKERQUE** 7NM, **CALAIS** 10NM

This town is largely a suburb of Dunkerque, but its well-preserved fort and walled town makes it worth a visit. It is the least industrial and most traditional of all the harbours on this stretch of coastline.

NAVIGATION

A lengthy, shallow entrance along a 1km (0.6 mile) breakwater. The entrance dries to a muddy trickle at LW. Access 2 hr either side of HW. Secure (locked) marina where deep draught yachts may touch into soft mud.

OVERVIEW

Like many towns hereabouts, Gravelines was heavily fortified during fighting between neighbouring countries, particularly when the Spanish held parts of Flanders. In the 17th century, it ping-ponged between France and Spain, finally falling under French domain in 1659.

The remaining star-shaped fortress from those troubled times gives the town its character, with the riverways and canals adding to the historical sense of the place. The river on which it stands is the Aa (pronounced Ar-Ar), and it is said that the water on one side of the fortress is salt, and on the other fresh. Because of the moat that runs all the way round the fortifications, it has a reputation for being the only town in mainland France with water on all sides.

▼ The first small boat harbour you come to dries and is for locals only

THINGS TO SEE AND DO

Hiring bikes here can be a good idea – there is no uphill, and good cycle tracks. The beach at **Petit-Fort-Philippe** is hugely popular and supervised, with changing rooms and games areas, shops, cafés, sand yachting and kitesurfing. Head for the beach to the east of the harbour entrance (50 min walk, 12 min by taxi, 20 min cycle ride).

▲ The harbour approach is much less daunting at HW

▼ Gravelines has maintained a strong sense of tradition in its harbour

The essentials:

FUEL 24 hr diesel at the marina.

REPAIRS There is no lift-out facility here but crane hire can be arranged – consult the harbour office.

LAUNDRY At marina, or Lav-Calmette laundrette, 59820 Gravelines (50 min walk).

MEDICAL Marina will advise. For emergencies, taxi to Dunkerque (30 min) or Calais (30 min).

The fortified town can consume an afternoon with **pedalo trips** and a **sightseeing train**. The lighthouse is painted in a distinctive black-and-white spiral and stands on the eastern side of the entrance. Open to visitors – 116 steps! Note that when the lock gate is open, it can be a 15 min walk into the town. Bike hire is available.

▲ Water on all sides of Gravelines!

FOOD AND SHOPPING

● **Lidl**, 1 route de Calais and **Super U**, ave. Pierre Pleuvret, supermarkets are within a 10 min walk.

● **Market days** Friday and Sunday.

● For a **fresh fish feast** try **Le Turbot**, 26 rue de Dunkerque. Chef Alain Coquelle's signature dish is **scallops** prepared in the shell with herbs and finely chopped leeks and mushrooms and sealed with pastry. Set menus starting at just 16 euros in a friendly and cosy atmosphere.

● **La Cave Gourmande**, 6 rue Léon Blum, is a not-to-be missed speciality food and wine shop selling **artisan foods** and **fabulous French goodies**.

● Seek out the prized **Merville potato**, which grows in the sandy soil hereabouts – easy to store and with a floury texture.

FURTHER AFIELD

The train station is a charming mix of brick and old woodwork, rue de la Gare (30 min). Connections to all stations in northern France but a limited timetable.

Tourist information
11 rue de la Republique
(20 min walk)

DUNKERQUE

HARWICH 65NM, **RAMSGATE** 40NM, **DOVER** 39NM, **EASTBOURNE** 80NM, **OSTENDE** 25NM

Dunkerque is a functional and busy harbour in an industrial setting with little in the way of charm other than in the old town, although unbroken white sandy beaches are a short walk away.

NAVIGATION

This is a large commercial harbour and a sharp lookout is needed in case of big ship movements. The entrance is easy, although rough in strong NW to NE winds. There are four marinas. The only two that require no lock gates or bridges to be passed through are the Port du Grand Large (municipal),

which is easiest for the beach, or the YC Mer du Nord (yacht CLUB), which is a shorter distance from the city centre.

OVERVIEW

● Anyone with a sense of 20th-century military history will know the story of the mass evacuation of Allied troops from the beaches of Dunkerque in 1940 in the face of the advancing Nazi forces. For an excellent overview, 10 min walk from the Port du Grand Large is the Museum **Dunkerque 1940 Operation Dynamo** – it's child friendly but allow 2 hr for a full visit.

▼ The marina is in a commercial part of city, but plenty of maritime tradition on display – the *Duchesse Anne*, the last fully rigged ships under the French flag

A fishing village in the 10th century, Dunkerque (trans: 'Church of the Dunes') soon found importance due to its position, and it has been at the centre of many conflicts, not least with the Dutch, Spanish and the English. It now sits in the Hauts-de-France district, of which the capital is Lille.

This is an important industrial city, and the third largest port in France. You may have seen the oil and petrol refineries strung out along the coast to the north as you sailed here. For this reason, although there is history here, and plenty of museums and galleries to reflect it, this remains a working environment, and given the position of the marinas you'll have to trudge considerable distances through bleak warehouse landscapes to find inspiration. The famous Dunkerque beaches, however, are close to hand and those with families may find these offer all they need for a good day out, and only a short walk from the boat.

The essentials:

FUEL At Port du Grand Large and YCMN during working hours, lunchbreak 1200–1400.

REPAIRS Seek marina advice or try Yacht-Services Dunkerque, 26 Place Charles Valentin (25 min walk).

LAUNDRY Self-service at 140 ave. de la Libération (15 min walk).

HIRE There are many self-service cycle hire points around Dunkerque. The tourist information offers pre-planned cycle rides for tours of the city.

THINGS TO SEE AND DO

The famous 'queen of the northern beaches', at **Malo-les-Bains**, is a short stroll from the boat and here you'll find 4km (2.5 miles) of unbroken sand, fringed with as many bars and restaurants as you could wish for. It is the most attractive resort on this stretch of coast.

▼ The houses in traditional style, some may have been rebuilt since the Second World War

▼ Now the third largest port in France with a workmanlike atmosphere

The **Musée Portuaire**, 9 Quai de la Citadelle (20 min walk), located close to the marina in the historic citadel district, has been built in an old tobacco warehouse, and gives a history of the city from a maritime perspective. The three-masted *Duchesse Anne* is alongside and open to the public, as well as the old **Sandettié lightship**. It's a major maritime experience.

See Overview (above) for details of the Second World War Museum.

FOOD AND SHOPPING

● **L'Épicerie du Grand Large,** 26 Place Paul Asseman, is a modest convenience store but the nearest at 15 min walk.

● **Market days** are Wednesday and Sunday in the square of Général de Gaulle. **Fish stalls** on the Place du Minck, not far from the maritime museum.

● For the widest choice of food, the restaurants that fringe the beach at **Malo-les-Bains** offer everything you

could wish for. **La Halle**, 103 Place du Minck (25 min walk), has one of the best reputations for a **fish feast**, and unless you book well in advance you won't get in. Make up your own meal from the biggest fishy pick'n'mix you'll ever come across.

FURTHER AFIELD

There is a regular ferry service to Dover but it's vehicles only and no foot passengers.

Fourteen trains a day leave Dunkerque for London (usually with only one change) with a journey time under 3 hr, making this a good place for a crew change. Rail connections to all major towns and cities in this part of France, also the Paris airports. SNCF station, Place de la Gare, 59140 – bike pick-up point here.

Tourist information
Rue de l'Amiral Ronarc'h
(20 min walk)

THE CHANNEL ISLANDS

MOST YACHTS HEADING TOWARDS BRITTANY from the south coast of England will, sooner or later, stumble across the Channel Islands.

If you were trying to invent a better stopping-off place on the way to France, you couldn't come up with anything. They make the passage to France far less of a flog; it's quite possible to get from, say, Torquay to Alderney without a night passage, and it's only 40km (25 miles) from Cherbourg. And once you're there, with only daysails you'll find yourself in some of Brittany's finest harbours.

▼ The Channel Island views change constantly with the tide. Braye Bay, Alderney

There is a price to pay, though, and the Channel Islands require some careful planning and well-timed sailing in order to enjoy, rather than endure, them. The tidal ranges are considerable, the currents are swift and fog is not unknown. But if you have the skills to cope with all those obstacles, the Channel Islands offer safe harbours and glorious rocky anchorages, all designed to get you in the mood for the Brittany waters to come.

As far as this guide is concerned, it is what you will find ashore that is at the forefront of our minds, and it can vary widely between the islands. There are five principal ones: Alderney, Guernsey and its close neighbour Herm all share a government, and then there's Jersey and Sark. Just to be clear, these islands are geographically part of the British Isles but not the United Kingdom. This can mean there might be more form-filling on arrival than you are used to. Also, expect the islands to have a different feel about them. They certainly don't feel like part of England, but nor do they feel like France, and each has its own atmosphere. As the French writer Victor Hugo said, 'the Channel Islands are like little bits of France dropped into the sea and picked up by Britain'.

BRAYE – ALDERNEY

NEEDLES 61NM, **DARTMOUTH** 64NM, **ST MALO** 63NM, **ROSCOFF** 95NM

Less than 6.5km (4 miles) long and just over 1.6km (1 mile) wide, many yachts speed past Alderney heading south. Don't! It has charm, and ancient and modern history, from Neolithic times to its importance in the Second World War. There is also half a dozen white sandy beaches and no danger of overcrowding.

NAVIGATION

The infamous Alderney Race sweeps past the island and strong winds against tide can be treacherous. Time your passage to arrive at slack water and don't even think you'll be able to fight the tide. The harbour is at Braye on the north coast and has no marina, but there are 70 yellow visitor moorings. There is good shelter here in SW winds, but anything with N round to E can bring an uncomfortable swell. But if you want to visit Alderney, which is highly recommended, this harbour is your only option.

OVERVIEW

As you might expect, the island has long been at the centre of a dispute between the English and the French, moving between the two. In more modern times, massive fortifications were built in the 19th century to try to deter the French, and Braye Harbour is part of those, although they were never finished.

▼ Hauled by diesel, the old carriages from the London Underground on the railway that dates from Victorian times

Even so, the breakwater remains longer than any in the UK. The entire population of 1,500 people was evacuated in the Second World War and when the Germans eventually arrived they found the place to be completely deserted. Jewish slave labourers were brought in to help construct Hitler's 'Atlantic Wall'.

Alderney has a rich history for such a small place. The few people who live here have an independent spirit; they will tell you they're not English, or French, or Guernsey people. Even so, you'll find French influences in their food and their names. The locals are called 'ridunians', derived from Alderney's Roman name of Riduna.

▼ You will pick up a mooring in the outer harbour – no alongside berths in Braye

The essentials:

CHANDLERY Mainbrayce chandlers sells gas and diesel (duty free) and usual spares. Crane available for lifting. Assistance given with repairs.

FACILITIES The harbour office is at the south-west end of the harbour. Close by are toilets, showers and laundry. For water, there is a tap close by the Mainbrayce chandlery and a tap at the top of the dinghy slipway. Mainbrayce operate a water taxi from the moorings.

HIRE Cycle & Surf, Les Rocquettes, St Anne (20 min walk).

THINGS TO SEE AND DO

The **Alderney Cinema**, 34 Victoria Street (20 min walk) is great for those storm-bound days, and is also part of the **Alderney Arts Centre**.

Alderney is a place for the simple things, so try **walking**, **birdwatching** and **snorkelling** in crystal-clear water. The tourist information can offer **planned walks** from the Coast Path Challenge, the Mid-Island Walk or the Gannet Trail, as well as explorations of the many **wartime forts and bunkers** (20 min walk).

Alderney Museum, on the High Street between Connaught Square and Victoria Street (20 min walk), has war memorabilia, lighthouse history, archaeology, history of the harbour and a hands-on natural history room for children.

There are no fewer than seven **beaches**: at Braye (white sand closest to the harbour), Saye (swimming in crystal-clear water), Arch (small and sheltered), Corblets (good for rock pools and surfing), Longis (wide and sandy), Clonque (rocky) and Platte Saline (shingle beach, good for dogs).

For such a small island, it's ambitious to have a railway. The **Alderney Railway** dates from the 1840s and was opened by Queen Victoria and Prince Albert and then operated by the Admiralty. It was designed to carry stone from the eastern shore of the island to build the breakwater and forts. These days a diesel engine pulls two retired London Underground Carriages along the line.

Bayeux Tapestry Finale – an Alderney Community Project – employed the help of 426 volunteers, including the Prince of Wales, to stitch this 3m (10ft) embroidery depicting the conclusion to the famous tapestry. See it at the Alderney Library, Church Street (15 min walk).

Boat trips are available to see the puffin colony on rocky Burhou, just over 1.6km (1 mile) off the north-east of the islands.

FOOD AND SHOPPING

It's an uphill walk to St Anne (note: not *St Anne's*) where you will find:
- **Le Cocq's Stores**, Le Huret (25 min walk). **Le Cocq's Bottom Shop** is closest to the harbour, behind the sailing club.
- For fresh fish, crab and lobster try **McAllister's Wet Fish Mongers**, Victoria Street (20 min walk).
- **Alderney Farm Shop**, Ridona Stores, Victoria Street (20 min walk).

- **Half-day closing** on the island is Wednesday.

FURTHER AFIELD

Direct flights from Southampton and Guernsey with onward flights to many UK airports. Seasonal inter-island ferry Alderney to Guernsey – The Little Ferry Company. Ferry Guernsey, Sark and Cherbourg in season – *Lady Maris II*. Passenger service (summer only) to Diélette, also via Granville from Jersey and Guernsey – Manche Iles Express.

Tourist information
51 Victoria Street (15 min walk)

▼ Not much a rush hour on Alderney – a decent walk from the marina to St Anne, but worth it

ST PETER PORT – GUERNSEY

ALDERNEY 20NM, **JERSEY** 25NM, **ST MALO** 52NM, **BRIXHAM** 70NM

Like its neighbour, Jersey, Guernsey is famed for its financial services, helped along by its tax structures. Thankfully, for the visiting sailor, tourism is also an important part of its economy so you'll find plenty to do on this island, which you feel you can almost hold in the palm of your hand.

There are two marinas welcoming visitors: Victoria Marina, which is in the main harbour and conveniently close to St Peter Port, and Beaucette Marina on the north-east tip.

NAVIGATION

Ensuring you are working with the tide, rather than against it, is the secret of successful Channel Islands cruising. The tidal ranges are substantial and anchorages must be chosen with care to avoid swell. There are offshore rocks aplenty.

St Peter Port

When entering the outer harbour, look out for a red light on the north pier, which indicates a ferry departure. You may be met by a helpful harbour launch. Head for the Victoria Marina – the 'middle' one – and make use of the waiting pontoon on the north side of the approach if needed (dries at low springs). You should be able to get over the sill +/– 2 hr either side of HW.

Beaucette

It's a narrow entrance with a natural sill and a useful tide gauge – it's a converted quarry. If there's any swell from the NW, wait for HW before trying. This place is a good option if St Peter Port is busy in high season, although room for visitors might be limited. It has a bigger tidal range than St Peter Port. Call CH80 to be escorted in, if you wish.

OVERVIEW

Like all the other Channel Islands, Guernsey is a place all of its own and not a diluted bit of England or France, so think of it as a 'not-quite-foreign' holiday. It's a proud place and they've been careful not to over-develop their tourism, so expect to feel a hint of time-shift as you go back a decade or two. Most activities centre on the coastline, with surfing, kayaking, fishing, diving and beach life aplenty.

The island is a self-governing British Crown dependency and its

▶ **1** Once over the marina sill, you're as close to the town as it is possible to be; **2** Careful attention to tides makes for a happy Guernsey stopover; **3** The Guernsey flag flying over the Loophole Tower No 5 L'Ancresse; **4** Much fought over down the years, expect to find plenty of fortifications along the coast. Castle Cornet, St Peter Port

1

2

3

4

parliament is States of Guernsey. Given its strategic position in the English Channel, it has been much fought over down the centuries and has been under both English and French occupation. Possibly its darkest days were during the Second World War, when the island was occupied by Germany from as early as 1940. You'll see many Second World War fortifications, as well as those from earlier periods.

Guernsey was once famous for its tomato growers, who took advantage of the mild year-round climate, although that industry is far less important now. The Guernsey cow is a docile and efficient milk-producing animal and its milk is rich and creamy. Be sure to try some. Alderney once had its own similar breed but it is now extinct.

Guernsey has a national holiday, Liberation Day, on 9 May.

THINGS TO SEE AND DO

Outdoor Guernsey, based on the west coast, at L'Erée (20 min by taxi) offers adventure activities with qualified guides giving tours and expeditions on the coastline, including abseiling, kayaking and a puffin patrol (April to July). Beginners welcome.

Port Soif Aby is a great family-friendly beach with a good café. Close by at Portinfer (15 min by taxi) is some of the **best surfing** – take tidal advice first because of uncovering rocks.

The **Guernsey Tapestry** (7 min walk) displays 1,000 years of island history in ten embroidered panels in an award-winning gallery. It's a quick and easy way to get a sense of the island's history.

Beau Séjour Leisure Centre, Amherst (20 min walk) has tennis and squash courts, a gym, sauna and a six-lane swimming pool.

L'Ancresse Bay is an excellent beach, and is well-placed for Beaucette Marina (20 min walk westwards).

FOOD AND SHOPPING

St Peter Port

- The **Victoria Marina** is as close to the town as it is possible to get and so a short walk will reveal most of the shops you might need. **Marks & Spencer** has a convenient Food Hall.

- **Co-op Locale**, in the Market Buildings, Market Street (3 min walk) fills most gaps.
- **Morrisons**, **Waitrose** and **Iceland** are on the island, but they're inland and require a taxi ride.
- The **Market Square** is just inland from the marina (drop-in gym and hairdressing).

FURTHER AFIELD

Condor Ferries has high-speed services from Poole to Guernsey (3 hr), Portsmouth (7 hr), St Malo (1 hr) and Jersey (1 hr).

There are flights to all parts of the UK from the airport (15 min by taxi).

Buses on the island are operated by CT Plus and there are frequent services to all parts of the island. The main bus terminus is on South Esplanade (8 min walk).

St Peter Port is the only harbour with a secure marina and a good place to wait for settled weather to visit other nearby islands, all of which are without harbour facilities but very much part of the attraction on the Channel Islands. Sark has deep-water anchorages on both sides of the island, which gives you a choice of shelter, although swell can be a curse. Famously, Sark has no cars and no running water but there is a highly regarded pub towards the centre of the island. Herm, opposite St Peter Port, has a few visitor moorings and settled weather anchorages only.

There are fast ferry services to both islands from St Peter Port. Herm is only a 5km (3 mile) trip – look out for the Travel Trident kiosk, which is to the south of the marina near the clock tower.

The Isle of Sark Shipping Company offers year-round services to Sark with a 1 hr travel time. The ticket office is at White Rock, to the north of the marina.

Tourist information
North Esplanade (2 min walk north from the marina)

▼ All the facilities of this thriving town are close to the marina

ST HELIER – JERSEY

CHERBOURG 50NM, **ST PETER PORT** 25NM, **ST MALO** 33NM, **WEYMOUTH** 90NM, **ROSCOFF** 80NM

They say there's more sun on Jersey than on the other side of the Channel. It's a rugged coastline, but with a safe and secure harbour at St Helier, the capital. Ashore, it's a maze of winding lanes, over 800km (500 miles) of them, and the highest numbers of car per head of population in the world. If you find the thought of cars off-putting, remember that nowhere on Jersey is more than 10 min away from the sea. A world-class zoo and good food – much of it fresh from the sea – make for endless entertainment opportunities for families.

NAVIGATION

If you're arriving here for the first time after leaving the UK, detailed attention to tides is required – the landscape is transformed between high and low water, and often you will be surprised, if not shocked, by what you have just sailed over.

There are two marinas on Jersey; head for St Helier Marina (the Elizabeth Marina is for locals). The marina is protected by an opening and closing sill, but access is about 3 hr either side of HW. There is a waiting pontoon (with land access) to port as you approach, should you need it.

▼ As you come round the pier head at St Helier, make sure you head for the correct marina – St Helier marina, the one on the right

▼ There is a waiting pontoon if you arrive early on the tide. Once inside, the town is close at hand

OVERVIEW

After 1066, the dukes of Normandy, whose territories Jersey was a part of, became kings of England. When that fell apart in the 1200, Jersey stayed on the English side. Even so, it remains semi-detached, having its own government, laws and financial arrangements, although it officially owes allegiance to the Queen. It is its attractive financial set-up that has provided much of the prosperity here.

Jersey is the largest of the Channel Islands, and like the others it has been the subject of much fighting between the French and English. In the 20th century it was the Germans who were the invaders. All sides have built considerable fortifications over the years and you may stumble across many of them.

Jersey lies only 19km (12 miles) from the French coast and offers mild winters and warm summers. It has its own currency – it's not legal tender outside Jersey, but if you return to the UK with a wallet full you should be able to swap it for British pounds at a bank. The language here was Jèrriais but it has declined in usage since the 19th century, although you might come across that too.

Good growing conditions have enabled Jersey to build a reputation for the luscious Jersey royal potato, and the Jersey cow provides the butter to dose them with and the rich, creamy milk to go in the tea afterwards. Woollen jerseys really do come from Jersey and were part of a thriving knitting industry, the first ever being knitted in 1837.

THINGS TO SEE AND DO

Jersey Maritime Museum is on the eastern side of the marina, so is a very short walk. Learn about Jersey's relationship to the sea, listen to songs and hear stories of pirates and privateers, as well as Second World War history. Historic boats are afloat in the marina. The museum also houses a liberation tapestry.

AquaSplash, rue de L'Etau (5 min walk) is an excellent swimming pool with leisure pool and activities throughout the school holidays. Great flumes.

Fort Regent Leisure Centre overlooks the marina from the top of the hill, and is unmissable because of its distinctive roof. It's an easy walk via Pier Road and a great place for families, with a playzone, quad bikes, gym, café, occasional cinema, table tennis and a pool. Full programme of entertainments in the summer. Opens early.

The essentials:

FUEL On passing between the pier heads, look out for a fuel berth to your right, on Victoria Pier.

REPAIRS Businesses cater for all manner of yacht breakdowns and repairs. Ask at the harbour office.

FACILITIES Well-appointed showers and toilets on the marina.

LAUNDRY On the marina.

HIRE Big Maggy's Coffee and Bike Store, The Esplanade St Helier (close to the marina) or The Cycle Centre, 7 Anley St, St Helier (10 min walk).

Channel Islands Liquor Company, South Pier Harbour, St Helier (10 min walk) runs distillery tours, with gin and rum tastings.

FOOD AND SHOPPING

- **Marks & Spencer (Food Hall)** Close to the marina.
- **Alliance Tesco**, 6 Sand Street, St Helier (10 min walk).
- **Co-op Locale Colomberie**, 22 La Colomberie, St Helier (16 min walk).
- **St Helier Central Market**, a Victorian market hall, requires a visit for cafés, fruit, veg, fish, bakery and meat. Ironmonger and bookshop. Great atmosphere (20 min walk).

FURTHER AFIELD

Fast ferry to Poole (4 hr 30 min) or the slower way by conventional ferry to Portsmouth (10 hr).

Manche Iles Express connects Jersey to Granville and Barneville-Carteret. Also to Guernsey and Sark.

Direct flights to many UK main and regional airports.

The bus services are good on Jersey, and a relaxing way to get to know the interior of the island. Check out the Libertybus. Start at the Liberation Bus Station (close to the marina) and makes plans from there. Bus stops are sometimes marked by the word 'BUS' painted in white on the road.

> **Tourist information**
> Inside the Liberation Bus Station in St Helier (close to the marina)

▼ The landscape changes dramatically as the tide goes out. Elizabeth Castle, Jersey

INDEX

A

Aa, River 136
abseiling 150
airports 18, 59, 73, 85, 100, 135, 141, 147, 151, 155
Alderney 69, 144–7
American Film Festival, Deauville 99
Anacreon, Richard 64
Ango, Jehan 117
aquariums 57, 63, 72, 130
AquaSplash, Jersey 154
art galleries see museums and art galleries

B

Barfleur 77
Barneville 65, 67
Basilique Notre-Dame, Boulogne-Sur-Mer 130
Battle of La Hougue (1692) 75–6
Bayeux Tapestry 90, 94, 96
Finale - Alderney Community Project 146–7
beaches
  Channel Islands 144, 146, 148, 150
  Coast of Finisterre 15, 16, 25, 26
  Cotentin Peninsula 63, 65, 67, 72, 76
  Côte de Granit Rose 29, 30, 31, 39
  Côte d'Émeraude 41, 43, 45–6, 50, 52, 54, 57
  D-Day beaches of Normandy 78–9, 83, 85, 86, 88–9, 92, 93, 94, 95, 98, 99, 104
  Normandy and Picardy Coast 107, 108, 114, 116, 120, 121, 124, 130, 133, 135, 137, 139, 140
Beau Séjour Leisure Centre, Guernsey 150

Beaucette, Guernsey 148
bicycle/e-bike hire
  Channel Islands 145, 150, 154
  Coast of Finisterre 17, 23
  Côte de Granit Rose 25, 35
  Côte d'Émeraude 43, 54, 56
  Cotentin Peninsula 63, 67, 72
  D-Day beaches of Normandy 93, 96
  Normandy and Picardy Coast 108, 121, 130, 133, 137, 138, 140
Binic 41, 45–7
boat trips 31, 64, 147
boatbuilding, Étaples 127
Boucane Du Grand Quai, Fécamp 112
Boulogne-Sur-Mer 129–31
Braye - Alderney 144–7
Brendan the Navigator 57
Brittany Walking Route 12
bus services
  Channel Islands 151, 155
  Coast of Finisterre 18, 21
  Cotentin Peninsula 59, 64, 67, 73
  Côte de Granit Rose 27, 31, 34, 36
  Côte d'Émeraude 47, 49, 52, 54
  D-Day beaches of Normandy 85, 87, 90, 94, 100, 105, 113
  Normandy Picardy Coast 110, 115, 122, 125, 128, 135

C

Cabourg 95
Caen 93–4
Cairn de Barnenez 24
Calais 133–5
Cap Fréhel 40
car hire 25, 33, 43
Carentan 80–2
carousel, Honfleur 104
Carré Rosengart, Le Légué 49
Carteret 65, 67

Cartier, Jacques 57
casinos 42, 64, 92, 98–9, 114, 132
Cathedral, Le Havre 110
Cathédrale St-Tugdual, Tréguier 33–4
Cathédrale St Vincent, St Malo 57
cemetery, Étaples First World War 127–8
Cézanne, Paul 103
chalk cliffs, Normandy and Picardy Coast 106–7, 114, 120
chandleries
  Channel Islands 145, 150
  Coast of Finisterre 17, 23
  Cotentin Peninsula 75
  Côte de Granit Rose 39
  Côte d'Émeraude 43, 46, 49, 56
  D-Day Beaches of Normandy 83, 88, 93
  Normandy and Picardy Coast 133
Channel Islands 60, 142–55
  chandleries 145, 150
  food and shopping 145, 147, 150–1, 152, 153, 155
  fuel 145, 150, 154
  harbour facilities 145, 154
  laundry 150, 154
  repairs 150, 154
Chateaubriand, François-René de 57
Cherbourg 60, 61, 70–3
children's activities
  Channel Islands 154
  Cotentin Peninsula 63, 64, 68, 72, 75, 76
  Côte de Granit Rose 27, 31
  Côte d'Émeraude 41, 45, 54, 57
  D-Day beaches of Normandy 98, 104
  Normandy and Picardy Coast 112, 114, 118, 130, 135
churches/cathedrals 26, 32–4, 57, 58–9, 61, 63, 67, 76, 77, 95, 103, 109, 110, 130

Churchill, Sir Winston
   98–9
cinema, Alderney 146
City Wall Herbarium, St
   Valery Sur Somme 124
Cod Festival, Binic 46
Côte de Granit Rose 28–39
   chandleries 39
   food and shopping
      30–1, 33, 34, 36, 39
   fuel 33, 35, 39
   harbour facilities 33
   laundry 33, 35
   repairs 33, 35, 39
Côte d'Émeraude 40–59
   chandleries 43, 46, 49
   food and shopping 41,
      43–4, 45, 47, 49, 50, 52,
      54, 57, 59
   fuel 43, 46, 49, 54, 56
   harbour facilities 43, 46,
      50, 53, 56
   laundry 43, 46, 50, 54, 56
   repairs 43, 49, 54, 56
Côte des Îles/Island Coast
   60–1
Cote Fleurie/Flowery
   Coast 79
Cotentin Peninsula 60–77
   chandleries 75
   food and shopping 61,
      64, 67, 68, 69, 73, 75,
      76–7
   fuel 63, 67, 69, 72, 75
   harbour facilities 63,
      72, 75
   laundry 63, 67, 69, 72
   repairs 63, 67, 69, 72
Courseulles-Sur-Mer
   88–90
Cross of Lorraine,
   Courseulles-Sur-Mer 89

D
D-Day Beaches of
   Normandy 78–105
   chandleries 83, 96
   food and shopping 79,
      82, 85, 86, 87, 88, 90,
      93, 94, 96, 98, 99,
      100, 103, 104–5
   fuel 81, 83, 87, 93, 96,
      103

harbour facilities 81,
      83, 103
   laundry 87, 93, 103
   repairs 81, 87, 96, 103
D-Day Experience 3D
   movie 81
Dahouët 50, 52
Deauville/Trouville 97–100
Diélette 68–9
Dieppe 116–19
Disney, Walt 80
Dives-Sur-Mer 95–6
diving 17, 148
Douve, River 80
Duchesse Anne, Dunkerque
   141
Dumas, Alexandre 99
dunes of Hatainville 67
Dunkerque 139–41
Dunkerque 1940
   Operation Dynamo
   museum 39

E
electric bike hire 35, 63,
   67, 93
Emerald Coast see Côte
   d'Émeraude
Espace Oscar-Niemeyer-
   Le Volcan, Le Havre
   109–10
Étaples 126–8

F
Far Breton 41
Fécamp 111–13
Ferme aux 5 Saisons,
   Flamanville 68
ferries
   Channel Islands 147,
      151, 155
   Coast of Finisterre 18,
      19, 21
   Cotentin Peninsula 67,
      68, 69, 73, 77
   Côte de Granit Rose 39
   Côte d'Émeraude 54, 59
   D-Day beaches of
      Normandy 82, 90,
      92, 94, 98
   Normandy and Picardy
      Coast 107, 110, 113,
      133, 135, 141

Festival du Chant de
   Marin, Paimpol 37
festivals 21, 37, 41, 44, 46,
   67, 76, 115, 122
Finisterre, Coast of 14–27
   chandleries 17, 23
   food and shopping 18,
      21, 23, 24, 27
   fuel 17, 20, 23, 25
   harbour facilities 20, 23
   laundry 17, 20, 23, 25
   repairs 17, 20, 23, 25
First World War 72, 126,
   127–8
fishing 15, 37, 41, 42–3, 45,
   46, 52, 62, 63, 64, 85, 96,
   111, 112, 114, 115, 122,
   126, 130, 132, 140, 148
Flamanville 68
Folk Blues Festival,
   Binic 47
folklore/superstitions 26
Fort de la Hougue 74–5
fortifications and castles
   41, 62–3, 65, 70, 73, 74–5,
   93, 108, 118, 129, 130,
   136, 144, 146, 150, 153
French National Sea
   Experience, Boulogne-
   Sur-Mer 130
fuel, where to get
   Channel Islands 150, 154
   Coast of Finisterre 17,
      20, 23, 25
   Côte de Granit Rose 33,
      35, 39
   Côte d'Émeraude 43,
      46, 49, 54, 56
   D-Day Beaches of
      Normandy 87, 88,
      93, 96, 98, 103
   Normandy and Picardy
      Coast 108, 112, 115,
      117, 121, 130, 133,
      137, 140
Funicular Railway,
   Le Tréport 121

G
Gold Beach 86
Gouët River 48
GR (Grand Rondonnée 34)
   12, 34

Grand Léjon lugger, Le
   Légué 49
Grandcamp-Maisy 81–3
Granville 62–4
Gravelines 135–8
Guernsey 67, 68, 148–51
guided tours 49, 54, 99,
   112, 124, 127, 150, 155

H
Henri IV Museum, St
   Valery en Caux 115
Henry I of England, King
   77
Herm 151
Honfleur 79, 101–5
Houlgate 95
Hugo, Victor 143

I
Île de Batz 21
Île de Brehat 39
Île de Tatihou 74–6
Île Vierge lighthouse 16,
   17–18
Îles Chausey 64
International Kite
   Festival, Dieppe 118

J
Jaundy River 32
Jersey 67, 152–5
Joan of Arc 123
Julius Caesar 126, 129
Juno Beach 88–9

K
Kastell Ac'h 18
kayaking/canoeing 17, 31,
   121–2, 124, 148, 150
kelp production 16–17
kitesurfing 137
Korrigans 26

L
La Chapelle des Marins,
   La Hougue 76
La Pauline lugger,
   Dahouët 52
La Vapeur du Trieux
   vintage railway,
   Paimpol 39
L'aber Wrac'h 16–18

lace-making 135
Landéda 16, 18
Lanilis 18
Laser Quest, Dive-sur-
   Mer 96
Latin Quarter, Paimpol 37
Le Grand Bunker, Caen 94
Le Havre 108–10
Le Légué 48–9
Le Tréport 120–1
Les Halles Médiévales
   de Dives-Sur-Mer 95–6
Les Jardins de la Mer,
   Courseulles-Sur-Mer 89
L'Estran cultural centre,
   Binic 47
Lézardrieux 35–6
Lieutenance, Honfleur 103
lighthouses 16, 17–18, 65,
   77, 138, 146
Louis XVI of France, King
   34

M
Maison Gosselin, La
   Hougue 76
Maisy Battery,
   Grandcamp-Maisy 85
miniature golf 31, 124
monasteries/monks 26,
   32–3, 54, 57, 58–9
Monet, Claude 99, 105,
   107, 109, 120
Mont St Michel 58
monuments and statues
   89, 128, 130
Morlaix 15, 22–4
Mozin, Charles 99
museums and art
   galleries
   Alderney Museum 146
   Benedictine Palace
      Museum, Fécamp 112
   Cape Horn Museum,
      St Malo 58
   Chateau-Musée, Dieppe
      118
   Christian Dior Museum,
      Granville 63–4
   Cité de la Dentelle et de
      la Mode, Calais 135
   Cité de la Mer, Dieppe
      118

   D-Day Museum,
      Corseulles-Sur-Mer 90
   Dead Man's Corner
      Museum, Carentan 81
   Ducal Palace, Fécamp
      113
   Duchess Anne's House,
      Morlaix 23
   Dunkerque 1940
      Operation Dynamo
      museum 139
   Guernsey Tapestry 150
   Henri IV Museum, St
      Valery en Caux 115
   House of Beurière,
      Boulogne-Sur-Mer
      130, 132
   Jersey Maritime
      Museum 154
   Juno Bravo toy
      museum, Le Légué 49
   La Cite de la Mer
      Museum, Cherbourg
      72
   Le Roc des Curiosities,
      Granville 64
   Liberation Museum,
      Cherbourg 73
   Marine Museum,
      Honfleur 104
   Maritime Museum,
      Île Tatihou 75, 76
   Musée d'Art et
      Traditions Populaires
      46
   Musée d'Art Moderne
      André Malraux,
      Le Havre 109
   Musée de Boulogne-Sur-
      Mer 130
   Musée de la Marine,
      Étaples 127
   Musée de la Mer,
      Paimpol 37
   Musée de la Ville,
      St Malo 57
   Musée des Beaux-Arts,
      Calais 135
   Musée des Pêcheries,
      Fécamp 112
   Musée du chocolat
      & Boutique Hautot,
      Fécamp 112

Musée du Vieux
Tréport, Le Tréport
121
Musée Picarvie,
St Valery Sur Somme
124–5
Musée Portuaire,
Dunkerque 141
Musée Villa Montebello,
Trouville 99
Museum-Aquarium
Maréis, Étaples 127
Museum of Modern Art,
Granville 64
Museum of Normandy,
Caen 93
Museum of the
Jacobins, Morlaix
23
Normandy Victory
Museum, Carentan 81
Onion Johnny Museum,
Roscoff 21
Satie House Museum,
Honfleur 104
Science and History
museum, Cherbourg
72

N
Napoleon 70, 72, 73, 126
Napoleon III 98
Naturospace, Honfleur
103–4
Nausicaà, Boulogne-Sur-
Mer 130
Norman language 61
Normandy, 1st Duke of
113
Normandy and Picardy
Coast 106–41
chandleries 133
food and shopping 107,
110, 111, 113, 115,
116, 117, 118, 122,
125, 127, 128, 132,
135, 138, 140, 141
fuel 108, 112, 115, 121,
130, 133, 137, 140
harbour facilities 112,
115, 133, 150
laundry 112, 115, 121,
127, 130, 133, 137, 140
repairs 108, 112, 115,
121, 127, 130, 133,
137, 140
Notre Dame church,
Granville 64
Notre Dame church,
Portbail 67

O
Omaha Beach 85, 86
Onion Festival, Roscoff 21
'Onion Johnnies' 15, 20, 21
Ouistreham/Caen 92–4
oysters and scallops 37,
41, 44, 61, 74, 75, 88

P
paddle boarding 17, 122
Paimpol 37–9, 41
Parc Emmanuel Liais,
Cherbourg 72–3
parks and gardens 57,
72–3, 89, 103–4, 124
Patrimoine Visites
Blockhaus, Fécamp 112
pedalos 138
Pegasus Bridge 92
Perret, Auguste 109
Perros-Guirec 30–1
Pink Granite Coast see
Côte de Granit Rose
pirates/privateers 50, 57,
153
Pissarro, Camille 103, 105
planetariums 26–7
Pléneuf-Val-André 50, 52
Plérin 49
polo 99
Port des Bas Sablons, St
Malo 55, 56, 57
Port-en-Bessin 86–7
Port Vauban, St Malo
55, 56
Portbail 61, 67
Portrieux 35
prehistoric monuments
24, 26, 41, 144
Proust, Marcel 99
public transport see bus
services; railways and
TGV
puffin colonies 29, 31,
39, 147, 150

Q
Quartier St-Vincent,
Le Havre 110
Querqueville 72

R
race courses/horse racing
97, 98, 99
railways and TGV
Channel Islands 146
Coast of Finisterre 18
Cotentin Peninsula 63,
64, 67, 73, 77
Côte de Granit Rose 24,
34, 36
Côte d'Émeraude 39, 44,
47, 49, 52, 54, 56
D-Day beaches of
Normandy 82, 85, 94,
96, 100
Normandy and Picardy
Coast 108, 110, 113,
119, 122, 125, 128, 132,
135, 138, 141
Regent Leisure Centre,
Jersey 154
Renoir 103, 105, 109
repairs, where to get
Channel Islands 150, 154
Coast of Finisterre 17,
20, 23
Cotentin Peninsula 63,
67, 69, 72
Côte de Granit Rose
25, 35
Côte d'Émeraude 43, 46,
49, 54, 56
D-Day Beaches of
Normandy 81, 87,
93, 98
Normandy and Picardy
Coast 112, 115, 117,
121, 127, 130, 133, 137,
140
Richelieu, Cardinal 110
river trips 29
rock pools 41, 146
Roman history 126, 129,
145
Roscoff/Bloscon 15, 19–21

S
Saint Ivo 33

Saint Josse trawler, Étaples 127
Saint Laurent, Yves 99
Saint Malo 57
Saint Tudwal 32–3
Sainte Catherine church, Barfleur 77
sand yachting 67, 137
Sandettié lightship, Dunkerque 141
Sark 151
Satie, Erik 103, 104
scallops and oysters 37, 41, 44
seal colonies 124
Second World War 55, 57, 65, 78–9, 80–1, 85, 86, 88–90, 92–3, 94, 108, 114, 117, 121, 133, 135, 139, 144, 145, 146, 150, 153
Siege of Calais 133, 135
sightseeing train, Gravelines 138
snorkelling 146
Somme Bay narrow gauge railway 124
sports/leisure centres 150, 153
St Cast Aventure - treetop adventures 54
St Cast le Guildo 41, 53–4
St Catherine's Church, Honfleur 103

St Helier - Jersey 149, 152–5
St Joseph's Church, Le Havre 109
St Malo 41, 55–9, 61
St Peter Port - Guernsey 148–51
St Quay Portrieux 41, 42–4
St Servan 58, 59
St Vaast La Hougue 74–7
St Valery en Caux 114–15
St Valery Sur Somme 123–5
St Vincent de Paul Church 110
steam trains 124
surfing 30, 146, 148
swimming pools 41, 45, 64, 72, 98, 114, 118, 154
  sea water pools 39, 43, 63, 108
  see also beaches
Sword Beach 92

T
Tabarly, Éric 42
theme parks 27
Trébeurden 15, 25–7
Tréguier 29, 32–4
Trieux River 35
Tro Breizh tour 32, 57
Trouville 98
Turner, JMW 117

UV
umbrella factory, Cherbourg 73
Vauban 55, 76
Vauban Tower, Île Tatihou 75, 76
Viking invasions 52, 61, 62, 72, 121
Village d'Art, Dives-sur-Mer 96
Village Gaulois theme park, Trébeurden 27

W
walking/hiking routes 17, 30, 34, 39, 52, 54, 65, 67, 92, 94, 133, 146
watersports 17, 25, 30, 31, 121–2, 124, 137
wildlife and wildfowl 29, 31, 36, 39, 124, 146, 147, 150
William the Conqueror 95, 113, 116, 123
wind surfing 121–2

YZ
yacht/sailing clubs 23, 56, 64, 67, 96, 98, 103, 108, 117, 133
zoo, Jersey 152

PICTURE CREDITS

(Top/middle/bottom = T/M/B, Left/Right = L/R)

All photography © **Paul Heiney** with the exception of the following:

Andree Stephan, Wikimedia commons: p144; **Getty** ©: p12, p14–5, p24, p40–1, p45, p46, p47T, p47B, p59, p60–1, p78–9, p95, 96, 97, p100, p101, p106–7, p109, p110, p111, p112, p113T, p113B, p115, p116–7, p118, p119T, p119B, p120, p121, p122, p126, p127, p128, p129, p130, p131, p132T, p132B, p134T, p134ML, p134MR, p134B, p136, p137T, p137B, p138, p139, p140, p141, p142–3, p145T, p146, p147, p149T, p149ML, p149MR, p149B, p151, p152, p153, p154–5; **Janet Murphy** ©: p55, p56, p57, p58T, p58B, p102, p103, p104, p105T, p105B, p123; p124T; p124B; p125; **Jean-Pol Grandmont, Wikimedia commons:** p114; **Sue Lane** ©: p98; p99; **W Bulach, Wikimedia commons:** p28–9

Maps by John Plumer and map data © Eurographics, 2021: p6–7, p8–9; p13